# 1st INFANTRY DIVISION
## 'Big Red One'

# 1st INFANTRY DIVISION
## 'Big Red One'

## Ian Westwell

THE
**MILITARY**
BOOK CLUB ★★

© Compendium Publishing, 2002

This edition first published by **Ian Allan Publishing Ltd**

ISBN 0 7394 2647 8

**British Library Cataloguing in Publication Data**
A CIP catalogue record for this book is available from the British Library

Printed and bound in the United States.

## Abbreviations

| | | | | | |
|---|---|---|---|---|---|
| AA(A) | Anti-aircraft artillery | | RCT) | MC | Motorcycle |
| AB | Airborne | CP | Command post | Med | Medium or Medical |
| ADC | Aide de camp | Coy | Company | | |
| AEF | American Expeditionary Force | DD | Duplex drive (amphibious) | MG | Machine gun |
| | | Det | Detachment | Mor | Mortar |
| | | D | DUKW amphibious vehicles | Mot Inf | Motorised infantry |
| AF in G | American Forces in Germany | | | MP | Military Police |
| | | DZ | Dropzone | Mtrel | Materiel |
| Amb | Ambulance | ea | each | OD | Olive drab |
| Arty | Artillery | Engr | Engineer | QM | Quartermaster |
| asst | Assistant | ETO | European Theatre of Operations | Pfc/Pvt | Private (first class) |
| A/tk | Anti-tank | | | Pl | Platoon |
| ATRL | Anti-tank rocket launcher | FA | Field Artillery | RCT | Regimental Combat Team |
| | | gren | Grenade | | |
| Bn | Battalion | HMG | Heavy MG (.50 cal) | Recce/Recon | Reconnaissance |
| BR | British | Hy | Heavy | RHQ | Regimental HQ |
| Brig | Brigade | Inf | Infantry | Sect | Section |
| Bty | Battery | **LCA** | **Landing craft assault** | (T or S/) Sgt | (Technical or Staff/) Sergeant |
| camo | camouflage | **LCI** | **Landing craft infantry** | | |
| cal | calibre | **LCM** | **Landing craft mechanised** | SHAEF | Supreme HQ Allied Powers in Europe |
| Cav | Cavalry | | | | |
| CC | Combat Command | **LCT** | **Landing craft tank** | Sig | Signals |
| C-in-C | Commander-in-Chief | **LCVP** | **Landing craft vehicle and personnel** | SP | Self-propelled |
| CG | Commanding general | | | Tac | Tactical |
| | | | | Tk | Tank |
| Cml | Chemical | LMG | Light MG (.30 cal) | USAAF | US Army Air Force |
| CO | Commanding officer | LST | Landing Ship Tank | USMC | US Marine Corps |
| | | Lt | Light | Veh | Vehicle |
| Col | Column | (1-/2-) Lt | (First/Second) Lieutenant | WN | Wiederstandsnest (resistance point) |
| Com | Combat (sometimes shortened to C as in | LZ | Landing zone | | |
| | | Maint | Maintenance | **Dates** | |
| | | | | 20/7/54 | 20 July 1954 |

# CONTENTS

**Acknowledgements**
A big thank you to the people who provided material, permissions and services in the production of this book: Donald Sommerville, Mark Franklin of Flatt Artt, Martin Windrow, Lolita Chizmar of Real War Photos (contact realwarphotos@yahoo.com or via PO BX 728 Hammond, In 46325 for copies), Teddy Nevill of TRH Pictures, Alan Butcher, Lawrie Bowles, George Forty, Stephen Dean and Tim Hawkins.

# ORIGINS & HISTORY

'No mission too difficult; no sacrifice too great – duty first!'

Motto of 1st Infantry Division

Below: Target practice with the Browning Automatic Rifle. The BAR was the main infantry support weapon of the AEF, around 29,000 being sent to France for distribution — each platoon received four to six. Weighing 19.5lb, of .30-calibre, the BAR took over from the French Chauchat that had been modified to .30-cal for US forces. The BAR would continue in service with US forces into World War II. TRH/National Archives

At 06.05 hours on the morning of 23 October 1917, a French-made 75mm field gun, serial number 13579 fired a shrapnel round against a German battery positioned close to the village of Rechicourt on the Western Front. It was the first of more than 10,000 rounds fired by the gun during World War I. To those Germans who saw or felt the round's detonation, the explosion seemed little out of the ordinary in a war dominated by artillery. Yet, the event was momentous. Number 13579 was not manned by French troops but by members of Captain Idus McLendon's Battery C of the 6th Field Artillery Regiment. This unit was part of the US 1st Infantry Division, the 'Big Red One', and heralded the arrival of American combat troops in the trenches that ran from the North Sea to the Swiss frontier. The United States had declared war on 6 April, but had a comparatively tiny army, so that few Germans expected the US would be able to influence the course of the fighting before they had decisively won the war. Battery C's action was a herald of the growing commitment of the United States to the conflict.

The story of the arrival of US forces at the front stretched back over several months. At the beginning of May 1917, the recently appointed commander of the American Expeditionary Force (AEF), General John Pershing, received a cable from Major-General Hugh Scott, the US Army's Chief of Staff. The brief message requested Pershing to select one artillery and four infantry regiments from the small regular US Army to serve in Europe. After discussing the matter with Colonel M. H. Barnum, Pershing selected the 16th, 18th, 26th, and 28th Infantry Regiments and the 6th Field Artillery Regiment to be the first US units to set foot on European soil. Initially identified as the 1st Expeditionary Division, they were later named the 1st Infantry Division.

## PREPARING FOR WAR

The first US troops to arrive in France, some 14,000 men, many of whom would form the backbone of the 1st Infantry Division, disembarked at St Nazaire on 26 June 1917. (The division did not reach its full strength until the following December.) The arrival of the doughboys was warmly welcomed in France and on 4 July the troops of the 2nd Battalion, 16th Infantry Regiment, were the guests of honour during a parade through Paris. A five-mile march through the city centre

took them to the tomb of the Marquis de Lafayette, one of the heroes of the American War of Independence, where Pershing looked on as Captain Stanton announced: '*Nous voilà, Lafayette*' ('We are here, Lafayette'). However, the festivities in Paris were short-lived. That night the marchers embarked in horse trucks for the rail journey to their headquarters at Gondrecourt, a few miles from the infamous German-held St Mihiel salient, where they began training under French direction. This was not a happy period for the division as both they and their hosts looked on each other with some bemusement. The French could not understand the unit's lack of basic training, while the doughboys did not appreciate the finer points of trench warfare. Reports reached Pershing of poor morale and lack of discipline and a visit to the incomplete division on 1 August seemed to confirm the facts as presented. He reacted in December by removing the division's commander, General William Sibert, and replacing him with Major-General Robert Bullard.

As part of the training of US units in France, they were sent into the front-line in supposedly 'quiet' sectors of the Western Front, often placed under French command, and given a taste of trench warfare. On the morning of 21 October 1917, the 1st Battalions of the division's four infantry regiments gained the distinction of being the first US units to come within sight of the Germans. They moved into the Sommerviller sector, some six miles to the northeast of Nancy; the enemy trenches were little more than 500 yards from the positions occupied. A few days later McLendon's Battery C announced their arrival. However, the division's troops were soon to learn the realities of trench warfare – the sudden wounding or death of comrades. The 16th Infantry's 2nd Battalion suffered the division's first casualties on 25 October and on the night of 2–3 November the deaths of the first three US

Above: AEF troops move up to the line. From 21 October 1917, elements of the 1st Infantry Division moved up to the French 18th Division's sector. They were affiliated for training, with this unit, the infantry and artillery training by battalion, one from each regiment. This continued until 20 November, when the division was withdrawn from the line. TRH Pictures

**1st Infantry Brigade**
16th Infantry Regiment
18th Infantry Regiment
2nd Machine Gun Battalion

**2nd Infantry Brigade**
26th Infantry Regiment
28th Infantry Regiment
3rd Machine Gun Battalion

**1st Field Artillery Brigade**
5th Field Artillery Regt (155mm how)
6th Field Artillery Regt (75mm fd gun)
7th Field Artillery Regt (75mm fd gun)
1st Trench Mortar Bty (12 med mortars)

**Divisional Troops**
1st Machine Gun Battalion
1st Engineers
2nd Field Signal Battalion
Headquarters Troop

**Support Services**
1st Train HQ and Military Police
1st Ammunition Train
1st Supply Train
1st Engineer Train
1st Sanitary Train (Amb Coys and Fd Hospitals 2, 3, 12, 13)

**Note:** During World War I US Army divisions were notably bigger that those fielded by other combatant nations. A division at full establishment consisted of some 27,200 men, approximately twice the number found in other armies. Each infantry regiment of three battalions had a full strength of around 3,800 men of all ranks. A brigade machine gun battalion contained three companies, each with 16 machine guns, while the battalion deployed at divisional level had four companies and a total of 48 such weapons. Each of the two field gun regiments comprised two battalions, each of three batteries, while the howitzer regiment consisted of three battalions, each with two batteries. With four guns to a battery, the divisional artillery totalled 48 75mm field guns and 24 155mm medium howitzers.

soldiers killed in combat were recorded. The losses were suffered by Company F near Bathelémont in Lorraine during a night raid by the Germans, which was heralded by a 45-minute box barrage that effectively isolated the section of trench being held by the company. Some 250 German troops stormed the company position. Fifteen minutes after they had entered the trench, the Germans departed, taking with them 11 prisoners. Three of Company F's men had been killed – Corporal James Gresham and Private Merle Hay had been shot at close range, and Private Thomas Enright had suffered multiple bayonet thrusts – and seven more had been wounded. The division was still raw and finding its feet. It was clear that more training was needed.

## THE BATTLE OF CANTIGNY

Bullard led the 1st Infantry Division back into the front line in the latter part of January 1918 as part of the French First Army under General Eugène Debeney. This did not especially please Pershing as he was under strict orders from his government that the AEF should fight as a unified whole under its own commanding officers, but as yet there were still too few combat-ready US troops in France to begin thinking of independent American armies. Nevertheless the division moved to the front. Bullard established his headquarters at Mesnil-la-Tour, a village roughly halfway between St Mihiel, the location of a dangerous German-held salient that jutted into the French lines, and Pont-à-Mousson. The division stayed in the salient until the beginning of April, when it was pulled out of the line and replaced by the US 26th Infantry Division. The question on everyone's mind was, when would the AEF really get to grips with the enemy? Training was only of any use if the lessons were put into practice.

Pershing needed to boost the prestige of the AEF and prove that it could form an effective part of the effort against the Germans. What he wanted more than anything else was a clear-cut US victory, something that would mean much more than just holding trenches in quiet sectors. The place chosen for the AEF to prove itself was Cantigny, a few miles from the town of Montdidier, a shell of a village that marked the farthest point reached during Germany's great spring offensive that had come close to outright victory. Pershing looked for a unit to carry out the attack and chose the 1st Infantry Division, which was operating with the French near Amiens. By 20 May, the division had been in the trenches opposite Cantigny for a month and had had plenty of time to appreciate the size of the task in front of it. The village, on high ground, was some 600 yards from the American trenches and every avenue of approach was swept by German machine guns and artillery. The French had already launched two attacks and on both occasions had captured the village at high cost only to lose it to rapid German counterattacks. To make matters worse, a major German offensive was launched on 27 May, the day before the division was to attack at Cantigny, and the ensuing danger to Paris led the French to remove much of the artillery and air support they had offered Bullard.

Despite this emergency to the south of Cantigny, some support was forthcoming – 12 French tanks, flame-thrower detachments and around 400 artillery pieces – and the US offensive opened on the 28th. The attack was led by the division's 28th Infantry Regiment under Colonel Hanson Ely and was directly supported by its 6th Field Artillery Regiment, machine gun battalions, engineers and two companies drawn from the 18th Infantry Regiment. The artillery began a full-scale bombardment of the German defences at 05.45 hours and one hour later switched to the creeping barrage behind which the assault waves advanced. Although they were heavily laden with extra ammunition and equipment, the infantry swept into Cantigny and captured it by 07.00, taking some 100 Germans prisoner after suffering around 50 casualties. However, any thoughts of an easy victory rapidly evaporated; German artillery began to pound the village's ruins and enemy infantry emerged from hidden dugouts to battle the doughboys. At 16.40, while the close-quarter fighting in Cantigny continued, the Germans opened a major bombardment and 40 minutes later their infantry counterattacked in force. The Germans threatened a breakthrough but Major Theodore Roosevelt Jr., the son of the former US president, led the 26th Infantry's 1st Battalion forward to plug the gap, and a further two counterattacks were beaten off. US casualties were heavy; by the morning of the 29th the 28th Regiment had suffered losses amounting to a third of its strength. By the afternoon the battle was over. Bullard later recorded the importance of his division's capture of the village at a cost of 1400 casualties: 'Cantigny, in itself, was a small fight. But Cantigny was, nevertheless, one of the important engagements of the war in its import to our war-wearied and sorely tried Allies. To both friend and foe it said, "Americans will both fight and stick".'

Above: The commander-in-chief of the AEF in World War I, General John J. 'Black Jack' Pershing (1860–1948) graduated from West Point in 1886. As a cavalry officer he saw action at the end of the Indian Wars — including those against the Apache leader Geronimo — and then served in the Spanish-American War, as an observer in the Russo-Japanese War of 1905, and in the Philippines until 1913, where he made his name against the Moro terrorists. He was chosen to command the AEF in France and fulfilled his function so well that his rank at the end of the war — five-star general of the armies — was given him permanently in 1919. *TRH/National Archives*

## SUMMER BATTLES

Bullard was essentially right – Cantigny had been a minor battle in Western Front terms. Such battles might be good for morale, but large-scale offensives were needed to win the war, and by the early summer of 1918 the vastly expanded AEF had the divisions available to undertake such operations. The 1st Division had the opportunity to take part in a large-scale counterattack in July, in what was known as the Second Battle of the Marne, a counterblow designed to throw the Germans back from the positions outside Paris they had gained during their spring offensives. The division had been rushed to this sector of the front to take part in the blocking of the fifth of the German 1918 offensives, which had begun on the 14th.

The Germans were halted within three days and the French immediately planned a counteroffensive to recapture the salient that the enemy had created between Soissons and Rheims. It was to be a joint US and French operation. Bullard was

Left: Troops of 16th Infantry Regiment await the order to advance near Visignaux, 16 July 1918. Two days later, on 18 July, the division would take part in the Aisne–Marne Operation, retaking ground won by the Germans in their Spring Offensive of 1918. *TRH/IWM*

**1ST DIVISION COMMANDERS**

Maj-Gen William L. Sibert from 8/6/17
Maj-Gen Robert L. Bullard from 14/12/17
Brig-Gen Beaumont B. Buck 5–13/4/18*
Maj-Gen Charles P. Summerall from
   15/7/18
Brig-Gen Frank E. Bamford
   12–18/10/18*
Brig-Gen Frank Parker from 18/10/18
Maj-Gen Edward F. McGlachlin Jr from
   21/11/18

*Temporary appointments.

promoted to take charge of the US III Corps, which comprised the 1st Division under its new commander Major-General Charles Summerall and Major-General James Harbord's 2nd Division. In the days preceding the onslaught the corps gathered in the vicinity of Villers-Cottêrets as part of the French Tenth Army and prepared to break through the western edge of the salient in the direction of Soissons. The attack opened at 04.45 on the 18th and the Germans were caught by surprise. Early progress was excellent but by day two the Germans had recovered from their initial shock and were fighting back hard. Their machine-gunners proved to be especially tenacious and inflicted many casualties, including the division's Major Roosevelt who was wounded in the leg. The division's greatest test came on the 20th during an attack on Berzy-le-Sec a little to the south of Soissons, which was held by the elite 1st Prussian Guards Division. The division's 26th and 28th Regiments advanced first in the afternoon and ran into a storm of machine-gun fire that cut them to pieces. Summerall ordered more troops into the attack and this turned the tide. The next morning the town was captured. The cost of the fighting had been particularly high, with the division recording 8,365 casualties, including more than 1,200 dead. The battle continued until 4 August by which point the German salient had been eradicated and Soissons had been recaptured.

## ST MIHIEL

By September 1918, the AEF's strength stood at more than 1.3 million men and Pershing was confident that it was capable of undertaking almost completely independent ground operations, although many artillery pieces, tanks and aircraft would have to be provided by the French due to the AEF's shortages of such equipment. The place chosen to test his belief was the St Mihiel salient south of Verdun which had been held by the Germans since 1914. For the attack, which was to open on the 12th, the 1st Division was allocated to Lieutenant-General Joseph Dickman's US IV Corps, which was positioned on the southwest sector of the salient. The advance began in appalling weather just as the Germans were beginning a withdrawal from the salient and, while their resistance was mostly patchy, the 1st Division had to fight hard to secure a small wood halfway between Seicheprey and Nonsard. Pushing north though the wood the division reached the village of Hattonchâtel during the early morning of the following day and linked up with the US 26th Division. In two days the battle had been effectively won. The salient had been eradicated and 13,000 German troops had been captured along with 460 artillery pieces.

## THE MEUSE-ARGONNE OFFENSIVE

Immediately after the success at St Mihiel the focus of the AEF's efforts switched to the north and west of Verdun. By this stage of the war German resistance was weakening and the Allies planned a series of hammer blows along much of the Western Front to finish the war. The US First Army was to attack into the wooded Argonne region and capture the vital rail junction at Sedan to the north as part of this effort. The 1st Division was held in reserve for the first part of the offensive, which began on 26 September, but was soon called into action, as the first phase of the advance quickly bogged down. The inexperience of the US assault divisions, the chaotic supply system, the extensive lines of German defences, the difficult terrain, and the dogged defiance of the enemy combined to blunt the US attacks. In

four days the US First Army had advanced a maximum distance of just five miles and the Meuse-Argonne Offensive was facing disaster. Pershing temporarily halted the operation to reorganise the AEF and plan a means of breaking the impasse.

On 1 October the 1st Division moved forward to replace the 35th Division, which had suffered 6,000 casualties taking Varennes on the right of the line of the advance of the US I Corps. Three days later, the second phase of the offensive began and the division was thrown into the fight for the eastern sector of the Argonne forest. As the fighting developed, the division battled successfully, though at great cost, to capture a pair of ridges in the vicinity of the village of Exermont and was then relieved by the US 42nd Division on the 11th. By the end of the month the US forces had fought their way through the strongest German defence lines and Pershing was able to plot the final stage of the offensive, the push on Sedan, which began on 1 November. For this operation, the 1st Division was initially held in reserve behind the forward units of the US V Corps in the centre of the line of attack. The German defences crumbled rapidly and the division joined in the headlong rush on Sedan. In its wish to be first to reach the town, it crossed in front of two other US divisions, a move that led to considerable confusion and anger in some quarters. Nevertheless, the 1st Division (and the 42nd) had reached Sedan by the 7th, although protocol dictated that a French unit had to enter the town first. Four days later the armistice came into effect and World War I ended. The division had suffered 22,668 casualties during its time in France and five of its men had received the Congressional Medal of Honor. In recognition of its extensive service it was awarded seven campaign streamers: Lorraine, 1917; Lorraine, 1918; Picardy, 1918; Montdidier-Noyon; Aisne-Marne; St Mihiel; and Meuse-Argonne. These honours reflected a record unmatched by any other division of the US Army.

Above: Casualties at an aid station. US battle casualties in World War I numbered over 264,000, 25,000 of whom died of disease. *TRH/National Archives*

# READY FOR WAR

**Right:** This photograph was taken in August 1941 — four months before the United States entered the war — as the division trained in the New River area of North Carolina. Here an early M3 Stuart light tank comes ashore from a lighter. *US Army via Real War Photos*

**Below Right:** This photograph shows the 1918 version of mechanisation with horse-drawn vehicles predominant. By 1940 US divisions had their transportation beefed up with 2½-ton trucks, jeeps, and ¼-ton trailers. A fully-equipped division had 1,440 vehicles of all types. *TRH/National Archives*

**Below:** Following the Armistice, the division advanced into Germany reaching Koblenz on 12 December 1918. It took up positions in the Koblenz 'Bridgehead' as part of the Army of Occupation, staying there until mid-August 1919. *TRH/National Archives*

As the 1st Division discovered after the Armistice came into effect on 11 November 1918, wars do not suddenly end, no matter how much the ordinary soldiers wish to go home immediately. After reaching Sedan, they had other tasks to perform, chiefly relating to the Armistice terms and the need to ensure that Germany adhered to them. General Peyton March may have authorised the demobilisation of the American Expeditionary Force on 16 November, but with some two million US troops in France and shipping in short supply, it was going to be a drawn out process for both political and practical purposes. On the 17th, the 1st Division was transferred to the newly created US Third Army, which had been earmarked to form what was known as the AF in G, the American Forces in Germany. Under this guise, the division made its way into Germany by way of Luxembourg. The border was crossed on 1 December. The objective was to occupy a section of the east bank of the River Rhine around Koblenz to ensure that Germany fulfilled the various clauses of the Armistice. The division had the honour of being the first unit to cross the river.

For the ordinary soldiers, their time in Germany was in some ways enjoyable. There was considerable fraternisation with the local population and most things were within the budget of a doughboy. However, the daily routine grew increasingly monotonous and most felt the pangs of homesickness. One positive development was that veterans organised the Society of the 1st Infantry Division and held their inaugural dinner, an event that continues to the present. Slowly but surely, the various AF in G units began to return home, but the 1st was one of the last. The Third Army was disbanded on 2 July 1919, but the division remained in Germany for a little while longer. However, on the 21st the division's headquarters arrived at Brest in France and a day later it sailed for home on the SS *Orizaba*. The passenger ship docked at Hoboken, New Jersey, on the 30th, and the division was given the first of two somewhat belated victory parades in New York City on 7 September. A week later it marched through Washington DC before establishing a temporary base at Camp Meade, Maryland, prior to the headquarters being established at Camp Taylor, Kentucky, on 29 September. The government saw no reason to maintain the US Army at anything more that its prewar levels and many of the men who served within the division were demobilised and the cadres of its chief components were placed along the eastern United States for much of the interwar period.

When Nazi Germany's invasion of Poland on 1 September 1939 led to the outbreak of World War II, President Franklin D. Roosevelt ostensibly maintained the neutrality of the United States. However, US foreign policy gradually moved to support for the Allies, most notably in the year after the fall of France in June 1940. By this time, the US government had begun to strengthen its own military, which had been greatly reduced in strength since World War I. In 1940, for example, the

## TYPICAL DIVISION ORGANISATION 1941

Headquarters, 1st Division
Headquarters & Military Police Company

16th Infantry Regiment
18th Infantry Regiment
26th Infantry Regiment

HHB Division Artillery
5th Field Artillery Battalion (155mm)
7th Field Artillery Battalion (105mm)
32nd Field Artillery Battalion (105mm)
33rd Field Artillery Battalion (105mm)
Artillery Band

1st Engineer Battalion
1st Medical Battalion
1st Quartermaster Battalion
1st Reconnaissance Company
1st Signal Company

Below: A 1943 photograph shows US forces moving up to the front — Kasserine — in Tunisia. While the German Army would end World War II with more horses than it had in the Great War, Allied mechanisation was effective and substantial. *TRH/US Army*

regular US Army numbered 243,000 men, the National Guard 227,000 and reserves 104,000. By mid-1941, the task of expanding, training, and reorganising the military was given to General Headquarters and its senior officer, General Lesley McNair, who would oversee its growth to its maximum strength of 2.2 million men.

The 1st Division was caught up in the strengthening of the US forces between 1939 and the United States' declaration of war on Japan following the attack on Pearl Harbor on 7 December 1941, and Germany's subsequent declaration of war on the United States. This period saw the division move between various camps in the east of the country. Among these were Fort Hamilton, New York; Fort Benning, Georgia; Fort Devens, Massachusetts. This period also saw the division commanded by three different officers: Major-Generals Walter Short, Karl Truesdell and Donald C. Cubbison. To bring the division up to combat readiness, it also took part in a series of manoeuvres, including the Louisiana Maneuvers [sic: US spelling] in the vicinity of Sabine during May 1940 and the Carolina Maneuvers of October and November 1941.

The division training for war was notably different from the one that had taken part in World War I. The US Army had been undergoing a major reorganisation, partly because the 28,000 strong divisions that had fought in 1917 and 1918 were found to be far too unwieldy. Rather than have two brigades, each with two regiments of infantry, they were given a 'triangular' structure that did away with the brigades and one of the infantry regiments. In the case of the 1st Division, this meant the removal of the 28th Infantry Regiment from its order of battle in October 1939, leaving in place the 16th, 18th and 26th Regiments. The 28th was reassigned to the US 8th Division in June 1940. The first stage of McNair's reforms produced a division of 15,500 men but a second round of rationalisation in 1942 did away with other components of the standard division to bring its strength down to some 14,253 men. New weapons were also provided, including the 57mm anti-tank gun and the 105mm

howitzer, and transport was beefed up with 2½-ton trucks, jeeps, and ¼-ton trailers. A fully-equipped division had 1,440 vehicles of all types.

Once committed to the war, the United States agreed to defeat Germany before Japan, a policy that was agreed with the British at the Arcadia Conference in Washington DC held in December 1941 and January 1942. As the first stage of this strategy it was necessary to begin shipping US units to Britain. This build-up, which was essential to any future plans for an invasion of Nazi-held Europe, was given the code-name of Operation 'Bolero'. The 1st Division was not the first US formation to land in Britain, but it began to make its way across the Atlantic from New York on 2 August 1942. After arriving in Scotland on the 9th it moved south into England, establishing itself at Tidworth Barracks in Wiltshire. The next few weeks saw the unit put through intensive training, particularly in amphibious warfare. The men did not know it but time was of the essence as the Allies had committed themselves to a major amphibious operation in early November. In late October, the division began to embark on the transports gathered in Scotland and speculation was rife as to the ultimate destination. Many thought Europe, but were wrong. Their mission would take them much father afield – Operation 'Torch' was to take the 'Big Red One' to the shores of North Africa. The 1st Division was about to become one of the first US units to fight in the European theatre of operations.

| INFANTRY DIVISION 15 JULY 1943 | Division HQ | HQ | HQ Coy | MP Pl | Ordnance Lt Maint Coy | QM Coy | Sig Coy | Inf Regt (3 each) | Div Arty | Cav Recon Trp, Mecz | Engr Bn | Med Bn | Total Div (w/o attachments)* |
|---|---|---|---|---|---|---|---|---|---|---|---|---|---|
| Officers | 38 | 2 | 4 | 3 | 9 | 10 | 7 | 139 | 130 | 6 | 27 | 34 | 687 |
| Warrant officers | 8 | | | | 1 | | 4 | 5 | 9 | | 3 | 2 | 42 |
| Enlisted men | 103 | 7 | 106 | 70 | 137 | 183 | 215 | 2,974 | 2,021 | 149 | 617 | 429 | 12,959 |
| Airplane, Liaison | | | | | | | | | 10 | | | | 10 |
| Boats, Assault | | | | | | | | | | | 14 | | 14 |
| Air compressor, Truck | | | | | | | | | | | 4 | | 4 |
| Tractor | | | | | | | | | | | 3 | | 3 |
| Ambulance, 3/4-ton | | | | | | | | | | | | 30 | 30 |
| M8 armoured car | | | | | | | | | | 13 | | | 13 |
| Sedan car | | | 1 | | | | | | | | | | 1 |
| Carbine, .30-cal | 104 | 8 | 44 | 55 | 102 | 148 | 148 | 853 | 1,871 | 99 | 66 | | 5,204 |
| M3 halftrack | | | | | | | | | | | 5 | | 5 |
| Machine gun, .30-cal | | | | | | | | 42 | | | 13 | 18 | 157 |
| Machine gun, .50-cal | | | 3 | | 5 | 13 | 6 | 35 | 89 | | 3 | 12 | 236 |
| Sub-machine gun, .45 | | | 3 | | | 12 | 32 | 18 | | | 30 | 16 | 90 |
| 57mm gun | | | | | | | | 18 | | | | | 57 |
| 105mm howitzer | | | | | | | | 6 | 36 | | | | 54 |
| 155mm howitzer | | | | | | | | | 12 | | | | 12 |
| Rocket launcher, 2.36in A/tk | | | 6 | | 5 | 5 | 5 | 112 | 166 | 5 | 29 | | 557 |
| 60mm mortar | | | | | | | | 27 | | 9 | | | 90 |
| 81mm mortar | | | | | | | | 18 | | | | | 54 |
| Pistol, .45-cal | 17 | 1 | 16 | 1 | 2 | 2 | 1 | 275 | 289 | | 3 | | 1,157 |
| Ride, .30-cal | 17 | | 50 | 17 | 31 | 43 | 45 | 1,990 | | 26 | 562 | | 6,761 |
| Truck, ¼-ton | | 1 | 16 | 15 | 7 | 6 | 19 | 139 | 82 | 24 | 16 | 9 | 612 |
| Truck, ¾-ton | | 1 | 7 | 3 | 5 | 2 | 13 | 12 | 114 | | 13 | 15 | 209 |
| Truck, 1½-ton | | | 7 | | | | 7 | 30 | | | | 2 | 106 |
| Truck, 2½-ton | | | | | 14 | 51 | 16 | 33 | 139 | 1 | 22 | 14 | 356 |
| Truck, 2½-ton Dump | | | | | | | | | | | 27 | | 27 |
| Truck, 4-ton | | | | | | | | 15 | | | 3 | | 18 |
| Truck, Wrecker | | | | | | 3 | | 1 | | | 1 | | 5 |

*with attached medical, chaplain, and band strength totals 14,253

## 1st INFANTRY DIVISION WARTIME UNITS

The following subordinate units were permanently assigned to the division:

Headquarters Company
16th Infantry Regiment
18th Infantry Regiment
26th Infantry Regiment

5th Field Artillery Battalion (155mm howitzer)
7th Field Artillery Battalion (105mm howitzer)
32nd Field Artillery Battalion (105mm howitzer)
33rd Field Artillery Battalion (105mm howitzer)
Special Troops
701st Ordnance Light Maintenance Company
1st Engineer Combat Battalion

1st Quartermaster Company
1st Signal Company
1st Reconnaissance Troop (Mechanised)
1st Medical Battalion
1st Division Artillery
Military Police Platoon
Band

### ATTACHMENTS

**Anti-aircraft Artillery**

| | |
|---|---|
| Bty B, 103rd AAA AW Bn (Mbl) | 12–15 Jun 44 |
| Bty D, 461st AAA AW Bn (SP) | 15–28 Jun 44 |
| 103rd AAA AW Bn (Mbl) | 16 Jun 44–7 Feb 45 |
| Btys B & D, 461st AAA AW Bn (Mbl) | 26–28 Jun 44 |
| 639th AAA AW Bn (Mbl) | 18–31 Dec 44 |
| Bty A, 460th AAA AW Bn (Mbl) | 1 Jan 45 |
| 103rd AAA AW Bn (Mbl) | 24 Feb–8 May 45 |

**Armoured**

| | |
|---|---|
| 745th Tank Bn | 6 Jun 44–8 May 45 |
| 747th Tank Bn | 7–13 Jun 44 |
| 741st Tank Bn | 7–15 Jun 44 |
| 743rd Tank Bn | 11–13 Jun 44 |
| 3rd Armd Gp (747th Tank Bn) | 11–15 Jun 44 |
| CC B (3rd Armd Div) | 6–30 Jul 44 |
| 33rd Armd Regt (3rd Armd Div) | 6–30 Jul 44 |
| 36th Armd Inf (3rd Bn) (3rd Armd Div) | 6–30 Jul 44 |
| 391st Armd FA Bn (3rd Armd Div) | 6–30 Jul 44 |
| 83rd Armd Recon Bn (3rd Armd Div) | 6–30 Jul 44 |
| Coys B & D, 23rd Armd Engr Bn (3rd Armd Div) | 6–30 Jul 44 |
| 87th Armd FA Bn | 6–30 Jul 44 |
| Coys B & C (3rd Plat), 703rd TD Bn (SP) | 6–30 Jul 44 |
| Btys A & D, 486th AAA AW Bn (SP) | 6–30 Jul 44 |
| Bty B, 413th AAA Gun Bn (Mbl) | 6–30 Jul 44 |
| CC A (3rd Armd Div) | 31 Jul–11 Aug 44 |
| 32nd Armd Regt (3rd Armd Div) | 31 Jul–11 Aug 44 |
| 3rd Bn, 36th Armd Inf (3rd Armd Div) | 31 Jul–11 Aug 44 |
| 54th Armd FA Bn (3rd Armd Div) | 31 Jul–11 Aug 44 |
| 67th Armd FA Bn (3rd Armd Div) | 31 Jul–11 Aug 44 |
| Coys A & C, 23rd Armd Engr Bn (3rd Armd Div) | 31 Jul–11 Aug 44 |
| 58th Armd FA Bn | 31 Jul–11 Aug 44 |
| Coy A & 3rd Plat, Coy B, 703rd TD Bn (SP) | 31 Jul–11 Aug 44 |
| Bty A, 413th AAA Gun Bn (Mbl) | 31 Jul–11 Aug 44 |
| CC B (3rd Armd Div) | 5–6 Aug 44 |
| 33rd Armd Regt (3rd Armd Div) | 5–6 Aug 44 |
| 36th Armd Inf (3rd Bn) (3rd Armd Div) | 5–6 Aug 44 |
| 391st Armd FA Bn (3rd Armd Div) | 5–6 Aug 44 |
| 83rd Armd Recon Bn (3rd Armd Div) | 5–6 Aug 44 |

| | |
|---|---|
| Coys B & D, 23rd Armd Engr Bn (3rd Armd Div) | 5–6 Aug 4 |
| 87th Armd FA Bn | 5–6 Aug 4 |
| Coys B & C (3rd Plat), 703rd TD Bn (SP) | 5–6 Aug 4 |
| Btys A & D, 486th AAA AW Bn (SP) | 5–6 Aug 4 |
| Bty B, 413th AAA Gun Bn (Mbl) | 5–6 Aug 4 |
| CC R (3rd Armd Div) | 8–17 Mar 4 |
| 3rd Bn, 32nd Armd Regt (3rd Armd Div) | 8–17 Mar 4 |
| 2nd Bn, 33rd Armd Regt (3rd Armd Div) | 8–17 Mar 4 |
| 3rd Bn, 36th Armd Inf (3rd Armd Div) | 8–17 Mar 4 |
| Coy C, 23rd Armd Engr Bn (3rd Armd Div) | 8–17 Mar 4 |
| 3rd Bn, 13th Inf (8th Div) | 8–17 Mar 4 |
| Coy C, 703rd TD Bn (SP) | 8–17 Mar 4 |
| CC R (3rd Armd Div) | 20–21 Mar 4 |
| 3rd Bn, 32nd Armd Regt (3rd Armd Div) | 20–21 Mar 4 |
| 2nd Bn, 33rd Armd Regt (3rd Armd Div) | 20–21 Mar 4 |
| 3rd Bn, 36th Armd Inf (3rd Armd Div) | 20–21 Mar 4 |
| Coy C, 23rd Armd Engr Bn (3rd Armd Div) | 20–21 Mar 4 |
| 3rd Bn, 13th Inf (8th Div) | 20–21 Mar 4 |
| Coy C, 703rd TD Bn (SP) | 20–21 Mar 4 |
| CC A (9th Armd Div) | 4–8 May 4 |

**Cavalry**

| | |
|---|---|
| 102nd Cav Recon Sqn | 11–13 Jun 4 |
| 38th Cav Recon Sqn | 12 Jun–31 Jul 4 |
| 4th Cav Gp | 1–7 Aug 4 |
| 24th Cav Recon Sqn | 2–17 Aug 4 |
| 4th Cav Gp (4th Cav Recon Sqn) | 12–17 Aug 4 |
| 4th Cav Recon Sqn | 14–17 Aug 4 |
| 4th Cav Gp (24th Cav Recon Sqn) | 11–30 Nov 4 |
| 32nd Cav Recon Sqn | 1–10 Mar 4 |
| 4th Cav Gp | 9–17 Apr 4 |

**Chemical**

| | |
|---|---|
| 81st Cml Mor Bn (Coys B & D) | 7–9 Jun 4 |
| Coys B&D, 81st Cml Mor Bn | 1–31 Jul 4 |
| Coy A, 87th Cml Bn | 1–31 Aug 4 |
| Coys A & D, 87th Cml Bn | 1–30 Sept 4 |
| Coys A & B, 87th Cml Bn | 1 Oct–17 Dec 4 |
| Coy C, 86th Cml Mor Bn | 13–23 Jan 4 |
| Coy B, 87th Cml Bn | 24 Jan–7 Feb 4 |
| Coy A, 90th Cml Bn | 24 Feb–10 Mar 4 |

| | |
|---|---|
| Coy B, 90th Cml Bn | 24 Feb–10 Mar 45 |
| Coy A, 87th Cml Bn | 30–31 Mar 45 |
| Coy A, 86th Cml Mor Bn | 1–12 Apr 45 |
| Coys C&D, 87th Cml Bn | 1–12 Apr 45 |

**Engineer**

| | |
|---|---|
| 20th Engr Combat Bn | 8–11 Jun 44 |
| 1106th Engr Combat Gp | 1–31 Oct 44 |
| 238th Engr Combat Bn | 1–31 Oct 44 |
| 257th Engr Combat Bn | 1–31 Oct 44 |
| Coy B, 2nd Engr Combat Bn (2nd Div) | 14–24 Jan 45 |
| 299th Engr Combat Bn | 24 Feb–10 Mar 45 |
| 1 Plat, 994th Engr Treadway Bridge Coy | 24 Feb–10 Mar 45 |
| 1 Light Equip Pl, 276th Engr Combat Bn | 24 Feb–10 Mar 45 |
| 72nd Engr Light Pontoon Coy | 24 Feb–10 Mar 45 |

**Field Artillery**

| | |
|---|---|
| 186th FA Bn (155mm howitzer) | 7–27 Jun 44 |
| 62nd Armd FA Bn | 7–31 Jun 44 |
| 18th FA Gp | 1–31 Aug 44 |
| 188th FA Bn (155mm howitzer) | 1 Aug–30 Sept 44 |
| 957th FA Bn (155mm howitzer) | 1 Aug–17 Dec 44 |
| 26th FA Bn (9th Div) (105mm howitzer) | 4–7 Aug 44 |
| 985th FA Bn | 1–30 Sept 44 |
| Bty B, 15th FA Observation Bn | 1–30 Sept 44 |
| Hq & Hq Bty, 18th FA Gp | 1 Sept–2 Oct 44 |
| 58th Armd FA Bn | 1–31 Oct 44 |
| 84th FA Bn (9th Div) (105mm howitzer) | 10 Nov–1 Dec 44 |
| Bty A, 987th FA Bn (155mm gun) | 1–17 Dec 44 |
| 60th FA Bn (9th Div) (155mm howitzer) | 6–8 Dec 44 |
| 955th FA Bn (155mm howitzer) | 13 Jan–7 Feb 45 |
| 965th FA Bn (155mm howitzer) | 8 Feb–10 Mar 45 |
| 193rd FA Bn (155mm howitzer) | 8 Feb–29 Mar 45 |
| Bty A, 987th FA Bn (155mm gun) | 24 Feb–10 Mar 45 |
| 188th FA Gp | 11–29 Mar 45 |
| 660th FA Bn (8-inch howitzer) | 11–29 Mar 45 |
| 951st FA Bn (155mm howitzer) | 11–29 Mar 45 |
| 957th FA Bn (155mm howitzer) | 11–29 Mar 45 |
| Bty A, 13th FA Observation Bn | 11–29 Mar 45 |
| Bty B, 13th FA Observation Bn | 30–31 Mar 45 |
| 951st FA Bn (155mm howitzer) | 30–31 Mar 45 |
| 980th FA Bn (155mm gun) | 30–31 Mar 45 |

| | |
|---|---|
| Hq & Hq Bty, 142nd FA Gp | 30 Mar–23 Apr 45 |
| 188th FA Bn (155mm howitzer) | 13–23 Apr 45 |
| 951st FA Bn (155mm howitzer) | 13–23 Apr 45 |
| 980th FA Bn (155mm gun) | 13–23 Apr 45 |
| Bty B, 13th FA Observation Bn | 13–23 Apr 45 |
| Hq & Hq Bty, 203rd FA Bn (155mm howitzer) | 28–30 Apr 45 |
| 191st FA Bn (155mm howitzer) | 28–30 Apr 45 |
| 734th FA Bn (155 gun) | 28–30 Apr 45 |
| 76th FA Bn (105mm howitzer) | 28 Apr–8 May 45 |
| 955th FA Bn (155mm howitzer) | 28 Apr–8 May 45 |
| Bty B, 17th FA Observation Bn | 28 Apr–8 May 45 |
| 186th FA Bn (155mm howitzer) | 1–3 May 45 |
| HQ & HQ Bty, 406th FA Gp | 1–8 May 45 |
| 200th FA Bn (155mm gun) | 1–8 May 45 |

**Infantry**

| | |
|---|---|
| 116th CT (29th Div) | 17 May–7 Jun 44 |
| 111th FA Bn (29th Div) (105mm howitzer) | 17 May–7 Jun 44 |
| 1 Det, 29th Recon Tp (29th Div) | 17 May–7 Jun 44 |
| 1 Det, 121st Engr C Bn (29th Div) | 17 May–7 Jun 44 |
| 115th CT (29th Div) | 2–7 Jun 44 |
| 39th Inf (9th Div) | 4–6 Aug 44 |
| 1st Bn (Coy A), 110th Inf (28th Div) | 18–22 Oct 44 |
| 47th Inf (9th Div) | 10–30 Nov 44 |
| 2rd Bn, 36th Armd Inf (3rd Armd Div) | 4–7 Dec 44 |
| 23rd CT (2nd Div) | 13–23 Jan 45 |
| 37th FA Bn (2nd Div) (105 How) | 13–23 Jan 45 |
| 395th Inf (99th Div) | 3–5 Feb 45 |
| 413th Inf (104th Div) | 21–23 Mar 45 |

**Tank Destroyer**

| | |
|---|---|
| 635th TD Bn (T) (Coy A) | 7–11 Jun 44 |
| 635th TD Bn (T) (Coy A) | 17–21 Jun 44 |
| 635th TD Bn (T) | 1 Jul–30 Sept 44 |
| 634th TD Bn (SP) (Coy C) | 1 Aug 44–6 May 45 |
| 703rd TD Bn (SP) | 18–31 Dec 44 |
| 3rd Plat, Coy C, 801st TD Bn (SP) | 18–31 Dec 44 |
| Coy C, 703rd TD Bn (SP) | 1–12 Jan 45 |
| Coy B, 644th TD Bn (SP) | 13–23 Jan 45 |

---

The following units of the division were seconded to other major units during the war:

Between 17 May–7 Jun 44 these units went to 29th Div: 26th CT; 1 Det, HQ & HQ Bty, 1st Div Arty; 33rd FA Bn; Coy C, 1st Engr C Bn.

Between 29–30 Jul 44, 26th CT went to 4th Div.

Between 6–23 Sept 44 1st Bn, 26th Inf went to 3rd Armd Div.

Between 5–15 Dec 44 these units went to V Corps: 16th CT; 5th FA Bn; 7th FA Bn; Coy A, 1st Engr C Bn.

Between 17–18 Dec 44 26th Inf went to 99th Div.

Between 6–8 Feb 45 these units went to 8th Div:

16th CT; 7th FA Bn; Coy A, 1st Engr C Bn.

Between 30 Mar–8 Apr 45 1st Bn, 26th Inf went to 4th Cav Gp.

Between 7–8 Apr 45 these units went to VII Corps: Task Force Taylor; 26th Inf; 33rd FA Bn; 1 Plat, Coy C 1st Engr C Bn.

Between 11–25 Apr 45, 1st Bn, 18th Inf went to 3rd Armd Div.

# IN ACTION

In April 1942, Britain and the United States established joint planning staffs to co ordinate future actions against Nazi Germany. Their chief focus was to prepare for cross-Channel invasion, but this had little chance of taking place until the spring o 1943 at the very earliest due to shortages of men and equipment. However, it wa deemed politically unacceptable for US land forces to do nothing against the Axis i Europe for a whole year, particularly as the Soviet Union was calling for immediat military action from the western Allies to relieve some of the pressure it was unde Initially, there were bitter disagreements between the British and Americans o what form any offensive action should take but finally a decision was made in Jul to invade the Vichy French colonies in Northwest Africa – Algeria and Morocco. Du to the political sensitivities of the Vichy authorities and their dislike of the British it was decided that the operation, which was code-named 'Torch', should have th appearance of being overwhelmingly US-led in the hope that resistance from th Vichy French forces would therefore be limited. Consequently, an American office General Dwight D. Eisenhower, was placed in command. Eisenhower had been i England since the previous June and had overall responsibility for the build-up of U forces in the country, which in July consisted of no more than the 1st Armored an the 34th Infantry Divisions. The final details of 'Torch' were completed on 2 September, leaving the planners just a few weeks to organise the invasion, whic was set for 8 November. One of the greatest worries that confronted the planner was the attitude of the Vichy French – would they fight or welcome the invaders?

## 'TORCH' — THE INVASION OF NORTH AFRICA

The build up to the operation was immense. From the United States came on convoy of 102 ships carrying the 24,500 troops of the Western Task Force unde Major-General George Patton destined to land at and around Casablanca, Morocco while a further 35,000 men were transported from Britain in 250 ships. Amon these were the 18,000 US troops, including the recently arrived 1st Infantr Division, which were to land around Oran, Algeria, and were known as the Centr Task Force. This task force, commanded by Major-General Lloyd Fredendall wa wholly American and also included the 1st Armored Division, 1st Ranger Battalion the 701st Tank Destroyer Battalion, the anti-aircraft 105th Coast Artillery Battalio and the 106th Coast Artillery Battalion. The remaining troops from Britain wer earmarked for Algiers and known as the Eastern Task Force.

Oran itself was considered to be too heavily defended to risk a fronta amphibious assault and three beaches were selected at varying distances from th

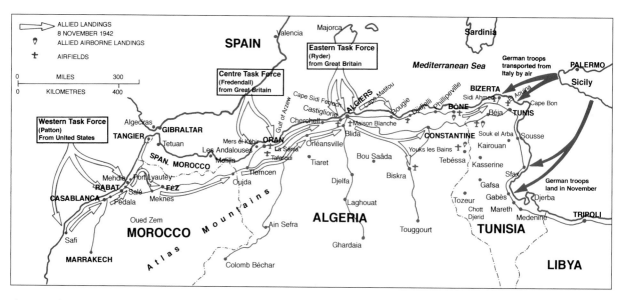

Above: Map showing the Operation 'Torch' landings. The 1st Infantry Division landed as part of the Centre Task Force, taking Oran with light casualties.

Right: Manhandling a 75mm pack howitzer on a crowded deck. *TRH/US Navy*

Opposite, Above and Below: Elements of the division came ashore at Arzew, near Oran. As these two photographs show, resistance was negligable. *TRH/IWM;TRH/UP*

port. From west to east, these were at Mersa Bou Zedjar, Les Andalouses and Arzew. Elements of the 1st Division were allocated to the latter two beaches, while an armored task force under Colonel Paul M. Robinett was to attack Mersa Bou Zedjar. Les Andalouses, some 10 miles west of Oran, offered the opportunity to outflank three powerful coastal batteries that protected the port, while the Gulf of Arzew was considered the best available site for a large-scale amphibious assault. Lying some 18 miles east of Oran, it consisted of a gently curving beach some three miles long backed by a sandy plain along which a good road ran straight to Oran. The assault plan called for landings close to the small town of Arzew, which was to be captured immediately and its two coastal defence batteries neutralised, then to put ashore tanks and armoured cars, which would push on Oran. Three Vichy airfields dotted around Oran at La Sénia, Lourmel and Tafaroui were also considered priority targets for the armour.

At Les Andalouses five transport ships, protected by the British cruiser HMS *Aurora*, contained more than 5,000 men of the 1st Division's 26th Regimental Combat Team under General Theodore Roosevelt Jr. These vessels carried the 26th RCT towards its objective, which was code-named Beach Y, in the last hours of 7 August. Exactly on schedule the ships spotted the beacon that was to guide them in and began to lower their landing craft at 23.20 hours. The heavily burdened troops had problems embarking on their assault craft but the first wave was ready to make the six-mile run to Beach Y by 23.45. It took more than an hour to cover this distance but on arrival the beach was found to be undefended. The only problem encountered was a sand bar a little way off shore. Three landing craft stuck on this obstacle and began unloading their cargoes of jeep and guns, which promptly sank in the deep water on the landward side of the bar. A way round this barrier was found and the second assault wave was arriving by 01.38 hours on the 8th. Due to the lack of Vichy resistance the large transports had moved to within two miles of the beach by 02.30 to speed up the unloading process and by 05.00 half of the 26th RCT was ashore.

Beach Y had two sectors, code-named Y Green and Y White and one battalion from the 26th RCT was assigned to each. Their first priority was to move inland a create a defensible perimeter. Shortly after first light, an anti-tank platoon had taken the village of El Ancor, which lay a mile inland and from where the road leading southwest to Bou Tiélis could be covered. It was here that the first Vichy armed response was met. At around 08.00 three armoured cars moved toward El Ancor and were hit by fire from the anti-tank platoon's 37mm guns and supporting mortars. The possession of El Ancor allowed the 26th RCT's 2nd Battalion to push eastward across the Plaine des Andalouses to clear Cap Falcon, where there were Vichy coastal batteries, and move on the Vichy naval base at Mers el Kébir, which lay close to Oran. This operation made good progress and by the end of the day, the 2nd Battalion was firmly established around the village of Ain et Turk between Cap Falcon and Mers el Kébir.

The 26th RCT's 3rd Battalion also advanced to the east but a little farther inland along the slopes of the Djebel Murdjadjo. After creating a fire base with a battery of 75mm pack howitzers and an infantry detachment, the battalion continued the advance on its prime objective, the Ferme Combier, which lay some 900 feet above

Below: The continuing buildup of forces around Oran ensured that local defences and shore batteries were quickly swamped. *TRH/IWM*

sea level on the eastern end of the djebel. However, heavy Vichy fire prevented the battalion from securing this objective. Nevertheless, the landing beach was secure and more and more equipment was being landed.

The division's main effort during Operation 'Torch' took place at Arzew. Here, 34 transport ships escorted by 20 warships of the Royal Naval arrived within five and a half miles of the landing beaches, code-named Z Green, Z White and Z Red, at 23.15 hours on the 7th. First in was Lieutenant-Colonel William O. Darby's 1st Ranger Battalion, which had successfully neutralised the defending coastal batteries by 04.00 hours on the 8th. The main landings of some 15,400 troops, comprising the 1st Division's 16th and 18th RCTs and an armoured task force on the three Z beaches would not be menaced by enemy fire.

Landing at Z Green at around 01.20, the 18th RCT had two main objectives – to relieve the Rangers in Arzew and push along the main road running from the town to Oran. The 3rd Battalion went to the aid of the Rangers and, despite some scattered resistance around the town's barracks and small naval base, the mission was accomplished by mid-morning. The 1st Battalion made initially good progress along the Arzew–Oran road. After advancing through the village of Renan, it beat off an attack by five Vichy armoured cars and moved forward to St Cloud a farther two miles down the road. Here, it was halted by a firmly entrenched enemy garrison supported by heavy artillery. Reinforcements were brought up, including the 2nd Battalion and self-propelled artillery, but an attack on the village was beaten off during the afternoon. A second wave of reinforcements, chiefly all of the 3rd Battalion bar one company left at Arzew, arrived shortly before nightfall and plans were laid to assault St Cloud on the following day.

Meanwhile, the division's 16th Regimental Combat Team had landed on Z White and Z Red beaches exactly on schedule at 01.00. Its 3rd Battalion, coming ashore on Z White, rapidly moved inland following a route to the south of St Cloud that lead it to the village of Fleurus some 12 miles inland and just nine miles west of Oran. While the 3rd Battalion was moving on Fleurus, the 1st Battalion came ashore at Z Red and immediately took two small villages, Damesme and St Leu, and then swung eastward along the coast road in the direction of La Macta some nine miles distant. La Macta was defended by Vichy forces and the 1st Battalion had to call in naval fire from HMS *Farndale* to help secure the village shortly after 12.00.

The action resumed on the 9th, although the landing forces were dogged by supply problems, in part because rough seas had prevented the unloading of vessels on the invasion beaches. The 26th RCT, advancing toward Oran by way of Ferme Combier, was not able to continue until the afternoon, and was quickly brought under heavy shell fire from batteries on Cap Falcon and from Vichy forces holding hills close to Mers el Kébir. The attack stalled. To the east of Oran, the 16th and 18th RCTs launched an attack on St Cloud. Advancing from three sides early in the morning, they fought their way into the village but were halted by stiff resistance by noon. A new attack was planned but the division's commander, Major-General Terry de la Mesa Allen, called a halt, deciding that St Cloud could be masked by one of his battalions, while the remainder would simply move around it and prepare for an attack on Oran during the 10th. Over at La Macta, the 16th RCT's 1st Battalion faced an attack by much-strengthened Vichy forces, some of whom were able to infiltrate behind the US positions. Urgent calls went out for air, ground and naval support but these proved unnecessary as the battalion beat off the French. After nightfall, it was relieved at La Macta and sent to rejoin the rest of the regiment for the advance on Oran.

The concerted drive on Oran, which involved armoured units and the 1st Division, was scheduled to begin at 07.15 on the 10th, although some of the

Above: Another view of the Arzew landings.
*TRH/US Army*

division's units had barely completed the reorganisation needed to launch th advance. This was spearheaded by US armoured forces from the south of Oran, bu the 1st Division's chief role was to advance into its eastern suburbs from aroun St Cloud. Despite scattered resistance, the armoured columns pushed rapidly int Oran and were able to link up with the 1st Division shortly before its attack on th eastern suburbs was launched. The local Vichy commander agreed that a ceasefir should begin at 12.15, but events had progressed so quickly that the 26th RCT di not receive the news for some time and was still battling around Mers el Kébir a hour later. The taking of Oran had cost the US forces less than 400 casualties.

Operation 'Torch' had proved a success, but it was only the first phase of a mor ambitious plan. This was to involve a rapid drive eastward into Tunisia, anothe French colony. Its capture would make any further resistance by Axis forces in Nort Africa extremely difficult as they would face an enemy on two fronts. Advancin westward, General Bernard Law Montgomery's British Eighth Army, which ha recently won the Battle of Alamein, was slowly pursuing the remnants of the Afrik Korps through Egypt and Libya, while the 'Torch' forces were to push eastward at a speed. The senior Allied command had high hopes of a quick victory but they wer not to be realised.

## THE BATTLE FOR TUNISIA

By the close of 1942, it was clear that the Allies would not be able simply to occup Tunisia. Due to a combination of bad weather, supply problems, difficulties i securing a definitive armistice with the Vichy authorities, German air power and th rapid build-up of Axis forces in Tunisia, the great advances from west and eas towards the Vichy colony following Operation 'Torch' and the Battle of El Alamei had stalled. Eisenhower bluntly told his senior American, British, and French fiel commanders on Christmas Eve: 'Gentlemen, we have lost the race for Tunis.' H concluded that the worsening weather would prevent any major offensive agains Tunisia until spring. His forces would have to hold on to the positions they occupied which ran roughly north to south through central Tunisia from the coast a few doze miles west of Tunis to a position a fev miles south of El Guettar. It was a lon line, some 250 miles, and the Allie troops were spread thinly along it.

Elements of the 1st Infantr Division, which often fough independently, had already bee involved in the failed battle for Tunisi by the time Eisenhower gave hi depressing summary of the campaign Shortly before Christmas th commander of the British V Corps General W. Allfrey, planned a push from Medjez el Bab south of the Rive Medjerda toward Tunis by way of Ksar Ty and Massicault. Led by the British 6th Armoured Brigade, it also involved the 1st Battalion of the division's 18th RCT, which was to support an attack by the

Below: American troops 'mop up a damaged blockhouse' while French sailors look on. *TRH/AP*

Coldstream Guards on the commanding 900-foot heights of the Djebel Almera, better known as Longstop Hill and only 25 miles from Tunis. The Guards attacked in appalling weather and evicted a battalion of the German 69th Panzergrenadier Regiment from Longstop late on the 22nd and handed it over to the 18th RCT, which was mostly forced off the heights the next day. The Guards recaptured the hill on Christmas Eve, but the Germans again launched swift counterattacks and regained possession on the 25th. In the few days of fighting the 18th RCT had 356 men killed, wounded or taken prisoner.

The winter lull was used by Eisenhower to begin the reorganisation of the Allied forces in Tunisia, which had become hopelessly intermingled during the drive from the 'Torch' beaches. It was clear that the British advance in the north was stalled and he opted to extend operations southward. To this end he ordered Fredendall, now commander of the US II Corps, to establish his headquarters close to the Tunisian border. However, Fredendall chose to occupy a position at Tebéssa, some 80 miles from the front, and awaited the reinforcements promised to him, including the 1st Infantry Division. However, while the Allies attempted their reorganisation, the Germans planned a major counterblow against the US II Corps. This involved two forces. In the south Field Marshal Erwin Rommel was to lead his veterans of the Afrika Korps through El Guettar and Gafsa in the direction of Tebéssa and by way of Kasserine Pass toward Thala. To the north, Colonel-General Jürgen von Arnim had the 10th and 21st Panzer Divisions. They were to drive through Faid in the direction of Sbeitla and then on to Sbiba. However, the two German commanders saw their objectives entirely differently. Von Arnim intended to inflict a bloody nose on the US II Corps and gain some more easily defensible ground; Rommel wanted to achieve a decisive advance that would break through the Allied line and then push northward to the coast. The attacks began on 14–15 February and quickly burst through the Allied lines, with many Allied soldiers simply abandoning their equipment and weapons. Within a few days, Gafsa and Sbeitla had fallen, and German units were at the entrance to Kasserine Pass. To the north the 21st Panzer Division was pushing on Sbiba. A major defeat was close.

At 09.00 on 19 February, elements of the German 21st Panzer Division moved against the Allied defences at Sbiba, which were held by the 18th RCT and the

**Opposite, Above:** M5 light (Stuart) passes infantry in Tunisia. *TRH/US Army*

**Opposite, Below:** Captured German SdKfz233 *schwere Panzerspähwagen (8-rad)* — heavy armoured car (eight-wheel) — mounting a 75mm howitzer. Used for close support, the SdKfz233 was introduced in 1941. *TRH Pictures*

**Right:** Soldiers man a jeep-mounted twin MG in Tunisia, spring 1943. *TRH Pictures*

**Below:** Soldiers trudge past a truck wrecked in battle. *TRH/US Army*

French Croix de Guerre with Palm, Streamer embroidered Kasserine

HQ and HQ Company,
1st Infantry Division
HQ and HQ Battery,
1st Infantry Division Artillery
announced in Department of the Army General Orders 43, 1950 (along with other attached units):

An elite unit, heir of the noblest traditions of the US 1st Infantry Division, which covered itself with glory during the war of 1914–18. Placed under the command of General Juin, Chief of the French Army Detachment, at the beginning of the Tunisian Campaign in 1943, distinguished itself in the Ouseltia valley, supporting effectively the French 19th A.C., and repulsing a strong German offensive. In March 1943, it received the shock of the enemy offensive at Kasserine, and after hard fighting, stopped the German armor and took successively Gafsa and El Guettar, at the price of great sacrifices. In April 1943, it strongly attacked near Beja and menaced Mateur in such a way that at the beginning of May, Mateur fell, opening the way to Tunis.

British Coldstream Guards. Both Allied units conducted a measured withdrawal which was covered by intense artillery fire, and the German armour blundered into the Allied minefields blocking their path and an attempt to restart the attack turning against some high ground to the east also stalled in the face of heavy artillery fire. Events elsewhere did not go as well.

At Kasserine, a mixed force under Colonel Alexander Stark, including elements of the 1st Infantry Division, came under severe German pressure as night fell. The attack by the German 10th Panzer Division was heralded by the scream of the new Nebelwerfer rocket-launchers and attacks by dive bombers. What followed was confused. As the US official history of the North African campaign recorded: 'What happened during the night of 19–20 February cannot clearly be constructed from the record.' Certainly, Company A of the 26th Infantry was surrounded and, as the official history records: 'the other companies went out of battalion control. Stragglers reported the situation after daylight.' What is clear is that the first line defences collapsed and troops – American and French – fled westward through the pass toward Thala.

On the 21st, the battle-battered Allied line, a hodge-podge of intermingled units, awaited the next German attack. The 21st was the turning point in the battle. Fresh Allied reserves, hastening south to bolster the line, heavy artillery fire and indecision among some German officers swung the battle in the Allies' favour. Rommel ordered a withdrawal, which was conducted with great skill. Following slowly, the Allies had regained most of the front line they had occupied before the opening of the German offensive within the week. However, Kasserine had taught them a sharp lesson. It had highlighted the need for many improvements in the combat training and to organise coalition forces to the highest degree. The lesson had been costly. Fredendall's US II Corps, some 30,000 men, had suffered 6,500 men killed, wounded or taken prisoner, while close to 400 armoured vehicles, 200 artillery pieces and 500 soft-skinned vehicles had been abandoned or destroyed. Yet for all the problems of Kasserine, the Allied forces remained in being and within a few months would complete the destruction of the remaining Axis units in North Africa.

Fredendall, who had performed so poorly in the Kasserine fighting, was removed from the command of the US II Corps and replaced by General George Patton, who set about instilling some order and discipline on its battered formations, on 7 March. On the 8th, the 1st Division was formerly assigned to II Corps. The Corps, with the 1st Division to the fore, returned to offensive action in late March, operating in conjunction with a drive by Montgomery's Eighth Army against the German-held Mareth Line in the south of Tunisia. On 16 March the division advanced as a unified unit for the first time, advancing east from Gafsa through El Guettar prior to attacking on the 21st. The battle opened with the 26th RCT and the 1st Rangers securing

e left flank of the line of advance, e Djebel el Ank, and then the bulk the division pushed forward. By e 22nd the division was holding sitions on a ridge of mountains nning south from the djebel and en westward across the road from Guettar to Gabès to the Djebel erda, which was held by two attalions of the 18th RCT. An Axis ounterattack led by the 10th Panzer ivision was beaten off on the 23rd ue to heavy fire from the division's rtillery. The 18th RCT recorded the efeat of the German armour: 'Troops arted to appear from all directions, ostly from tanks. Hit anti-tank ompany and 3rd Battalion. Our rtillery crucified them with high xplosive shells and they were falling ke flies. Tanks seem to be moving the rear; those that could move.' he two battalions of the 18th RCT n the Djebel Berda were forced withdraw two miles during the 5th but blocked any further erman movement. Despite these arly advances, the Allied push abès was brought to an end on April.

Following a redeployment of the S II Corps to northern Tunisia, the ivision took over from the British th Division at Beja on 16 April and ttacked in the direction of the line of e highway running between Medjez Bab and Tunis on the 22nd. The key bjective was a ragged jumble of hills eparating the Djoumine and Tine ivers. The 18th RCT cleared Hill 407. he 26th RCT captured Hill 575 and eached the Djebel el Anz in the face

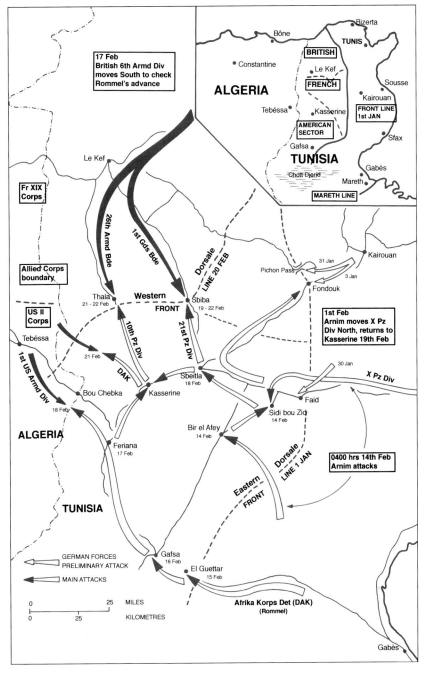

f stiff German resistance on the 28th, while the 16th Regiment temporarily took ill 523 on 1 May. The German defences seemed in tatters and it looked possible hat the US 1st Armored Division would be able to push into the open terrain eyond the hills, but vicious German counterattacks prevented any immediate xploitation. However, the decisive breakthrough came elsewhere and the defeat of he Axis forces in Tunisia followed within two weeks. The formal surrender came on 3 May and 200,000 Axis troops went into captivity. For the 1st Division the fight r North Africa was over, but it marked only the end of one chapter of its war gainst the Axis forces in Europe.

Above: Tunisian front line as at 1 January 1943 and the Battle of Kasserine.

Left: Engineers prepare rail lines at Kasserine after the battle. *TRH/US Army*

# OPERATION 'HUSKY' — THE INVASION OF SICILY

The defeat of the Axis forces in North Africa in May 1943 heightened disagreemen between the British and US military planners concerning the Western Allies' futu war strategy. At the Casablanca conference, which had been held the previo January, the British argued for an invasion of Italian territory, while the America believed that Germany was the main enemy and had to be defeated before the w could be won. To them, Italy seemed a side-show, one that might suck in resourc better employed elsewhere. While this latter view was essentially correct, the Briti stated, equally correctly, that an all-out invasion of the European mainland w totally out of the question in 1943 because the means of doing so, not least t landing craft and amphibious assault equipment required, were still not available sufficient quantities. A compromise was agreed. Sicily was to be invaded, possi as a prelude to an assault on the Italian mainland, but the main effort was to reserved for a later invasion of France. On the plus side the Sicily campaign wou probably draw German forces away from the proposed invasion sites in northe Europe, likely lead to the overthrow of Mussolini, and demonstrate to Russia th the Western Allies were making a significant contribution to the war.

The invasion, which was given the code-name Operation 'Husky', was schedul to begin in the second week of July, and the final details were agreed on 13 May. Tl Allies committed the two armies of General Harold Alexander's 15th Army Group the operation: General Bernard Montgomery's Anglo-Canadian Eighth Army was assault the southeast of the island, while General George Patton's US Seventh Arn was to land on the southwest shore. Once ashore the British were to push direct northward for Messina, the island's capital and key objective, while Patton was drive on Palermo on the northwest coast. In both sectors, paratrooper assaults we to precede the main landings. The 1st Division, which had embarked from Algeria part of General Omar Bradley's US II Corps under Patton and was part of the fir assault wave, joined an invasion force comprising 2,500 ships of all types a 160,000 troops. Opposing them on Sicily were the 230,000 troops of varying quali of General Alfredo Guzzoni's Italian Sixth Army and 40,000 Germans, the latt nominally under Italian command but taking their orders from General Albe Kesselring. The various Allied forces gathered off the west and east coasts of Mal on 9 July and landed on Sicily during the early hours of the following day.

The beaches to be assaulted by Bradley's corps lay along the southwest coast the island, stretching some 40 miles from Licata to Scoglitti; the 1st Division, le

Below: Independence Day — 4 July — 1943: the harbour at Mers el Kébir bustles with Allied warships preparing for the invasion of Sicily. Three years earlier, between 3 and 5 July 1940, it was against French naval ships in Mers el Kébir that the Royal Navy unleashed Operation 'Catapult'. The sinking of French vessels and the great loss of life were reasons why Vichy French resistance was somewhat stronger than anticipated. The trio of destroyers are of the RN's 'Q' class — G09 is *Quilliam*, G70 *Queenborough* and G45 *Quail*, which was mined off Calabria on 15 November 1943 and would eventually founder while on tow between Bari and Taranto the next year. *TRH Pictures*

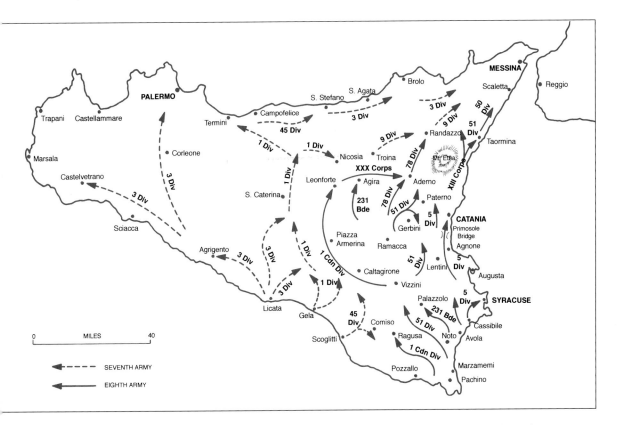

Above: Operation 'Husky' showing the massive operation launched on 10 July 1943, two months after the fall of Axis forces in North Africa. The 1st Infantry Division was involved in serious fighting at Gela on 11 and 12 July when the Axis forces committed the better part of two divisions — the Hermann Göring Division and the Italian Livorno Division. Backed up with heavy air attacks by Italian and German aircraft from Italy, it took a courageous defence and naval gunfire to repel the attacks. Just over a month later Sicily had fallen.

one of its regimental combat teams which was the army's floating reserve, was to land directly in the centre of the Bay of Gela, against the small port of Gela itself, on what was code-named Dime Beach. The 1st Division's immediate objectives were to aid recently landed US paratrooper forces at Piano Lupo, take two airfields at Gela-Farello and Ponte Olivo and occupy Niscemi. The airfields were particularly important as Allied aircraft operating from them would be able to fly support missions for the ground troops pushing into the island's mountainous interior.

The opening operations by Allied airborne forces sowed confusion in the mind of the Axis commander during the early hours of the 10th but also alerted him to the immediate likelihood of a major amphibious assault. Orders went out to the units under his command to take up position close to the most likely invasion beaches, with the paratroopers of the Hermann Göring Panzer Division being directed to mass along the high ground to the northeast of Gela prior to advancing against the coast. Elsewhere, the Italian Livorno Division lay to the northwest, and two other Italian mobile forces, known as E and H, were in the vicinity. Although the division faced only the second-string Italian XVIII Coastal Brigade on landing, beyond lay some of the best Axis forces on the island, including the Hermann Göring Division under Major-General Paul Conrath.

The opening amphibious assault went almost to plan, despite a storm on 9 July that threatened the timetable and made many of the troops seasick. Following a lightning assault by US Rangers, which neutralised an Italian coastal battery and secured Gela, the division's 16th and 26th Regimental Combat Teams came ashore in some 200 landing craft almost on schedule in the face of sporadic fire from machine guns and artillery. By 09.00 hours Gela-Farello airfield had fallen to the 26th RCT, which was pushing along Highway 117 toward Ponte Olivo, while the 16th RCT had linked up with the US paratroopers positioned around Piano Lupo.

**Right:** The convoy to Sicily was as big as anything seen in the war — eight divisions were involved in the initial assault. During the journey, 40mph winds caused real problems for smaller craft and played havoc with the air-dropping of US paratroops — the 82nd Airborne — and British glider-borne forces. The photograph shows part of the Western Naval Task Force (under American Vice Admiral H. Kent Hewitt). *TRH/US Navy*

**Below Right:** Patton was an aggressive dynamic commander the size of whose ego was matched only by his abilities. The incidents in Sicily almost lost the Allies one of their best commanders, but Patton would perform brilliantly in France with the US Third Army. This photograph is from that later period, dated 26 August 1944. *TRH/US Army*

The commander of the Hermann Göring Division, Conrath, asked for and was granted permission to move against Gela. His plan was to push southward toward Biscari and Niscemi from his forming-up area at Caltagirone and then strike westward against the eastern side of the 1st Division's beachhead perimeter. The division began to move forward at 04.00 hours. However, due to poor roads, sorties by Allied ground-attack aircraft and resistance offered by scattered groups of paratroopers from the US 82nd Airborne Division, Conrath's force, two heavily reinforced regiments, was unable to attack until after 14.00 hours. Aided by naval bombardment, the 1st Infantry Division beat off two main attacks and at 16.00 hours Conrath pulled back.

The Germans, with support from the Italian Livorno Division under General Domenico Chirieleison, launched much more determined and co-ordinated attacks during the following day, the 11th. Conrath moved three columns of his division against the 1st Division beachhead from the northeast, while the Livorno Division attacked from the northwest. These advances began at around 06.00 hours, with the focus of the attack being down Highway 117 in the direction of Ponte Olivo and the 26th RCT. The fighting was at very close range, much of it among sand dunes, with the German armour reaching to within 2,000 yards of the shoreline. Supply dumps and landing craft were hit and Conrath reported to Guzzoni that 'Pressure by the Hermann Göring Division has forced the enemy to re-embark temporarily.'

Conrath's message proved premature; there was no question of the 1st Division withdrawing. Allied warships had to remain silent for fear of hitting their own troops as the fighting was at such close ranges but anti-tank guns, bazookas and grenades used at close range prevented the Germans from advancing across the coast road. By 14.00 hours the German thrusts, too, were beaten back with heavy losses, despite the 1st Division being almost wholly without tank support. Some 40 of the 60 German tanks unleashed across the plain of Gela by Conrath against the 1st Infantry Division were destroyed, in part by naval gunfire, chiefly from the cruiser USS *Boise*, and the arrival of some tank support. The German commander was forced to make a staged withdrawal back to Caltagirone by way of Niscemi, although the 1st Division still faced stiff fighting around Piano Lupo. To the northwest the Livorno Division suffered a similar fate on the 11th. Supported by naval gunfire, the invaders smashed its attacks and took some 600 prisoners. However, Patton, who watched the day's fighting from a convenient two-storey building in Gela, was not happy with the rate of progress of his forces. He ordered the 1st Division's

# PATTON AND THE SLAPPING INCIDENTS

During the middle of the Sicilian campaign, General George Patton paid a visit to the 1st Infantry Division. A strict disciplinarian he believed that the unit needed galvanising, particularly as he thought its commander, General Terry de la Mesa Allen, and his deputy, General Theodore Roosevelt, Jr., were not pushing their troops hard enough. During the visit Patton was informed by the divisional surgeon that many men were showing increasing signs of combat fatigue. Patton would not countenance such talk and believed that combat fatigue was no more than cowardice.

The following day, 3 August, Patton stopped off at the 15th Evacuation Hospital near Nicosia, where he was shown around the facilities. At one point he stopped in front of Private Charles Kuhl of the 1st Division's 26th Infantry Regiment, who was wearing a tag, which recorded his condition as 'psycho-neurosis anxiety; state – moderate severe'. Asked by the general what was wrong, the soldier replied: 'I guess I can't take it.' At this Patton flew into a rage, slapped the soldier across the face with his gloves, and then threw him out of the tent. That evening Patton drafted a memorandum to his field commanders stating that: 'You will take measures to see that such cases are not sent to the hospital, but are dealt with in their units. Those who are not willing to fight will be tried by court martial for cowardice in the face of the enemy.' (Kuhl was later diagnosed as having chronic dysentery and malaria, and was shipped to North Africa for treatment.)

A second incident occurred on the 10th at the 93rd Evacuation Hospital, this time involving Private Paul Bennett of the 13th Field Artillery. When asked by Patton what the matter was, Bennett replied: 'It's my nerves.' Again Patton flew into a rage pulled out a pistol threatening to shoot, and finally slapped Bennett across the face. The general made to leave the tent but returned and slapped the soldier again. The hospital commander, Colonel Donald Currier, reported the incident and a copy of this found its way through medical channels to General Eisenhower on the 16th. Eisenhower did not want to lose a commander as valuable as Patton, but he could not avoid censuring his behaviour.

On receiving Eisenhower's note concerning the events, Patton set out to make amends. He apologised to the soldiers concerned and the medical personnel present during the incidents. More remarkably, he addressed all of the divisions of the Seventh Army in turn, apologizing 'for any occasions, when I may have harshly criticised individuals'. The reception he received was mixed and it has been reported that he was met with stony silence by the 1st Division. Eisenhower accepted the sincerity of Patton's apologies and decided to take the matter no further. However, news of the incidents reached the press in the United States and Patton's actions were generally viewed in a harsh light by the public. He did not return to front-line action until shortly after the Normandy landings and with General Omar Bradley, his subordinate in Sicily, as his commander.

**Above:** Training for the invasion of Sicily — 18th Infantry Regiment at Port aux Poules near Oran, 5 June 1943. *US Army via Real War Photos*

**Left:** US forces make their way through the timeless Sicilian countryside. The campaign was a remarkable success, although the Germans and Italians were able to save the bulk of their forces — over 100,000 men, 10,000 vehicles and nearly 50 tanks — in a desperate retreat over the Messina Straits. *TRH/US National Archives*

**Above Right:** A DUKW carrying cases of .50-cal ammunition for shore near Gela. The DUKW was developed during 1941–42 and an initial US Army order for 2,000 units was ratified in October 1942. Over 21,000 DUKWs were eventually built — 4,500 in 1943 — and it saw its first use in March 1943 in Noumea in the Pacific. Its first use in Europe was during the invasion of Sicily *TRH/US Air Force*

**Right:** Loaded LCM leaves USS *Leonard Wood* for the beach, 10 July 1943, seen over a three-inch gun position. *TRH/US National Archives*

Above: The attack of Sicily was the last battle that the 1st Infantry would fight in the Mediterranean theatre. While many saw the escape of so many Axis soldiers as a missed opportunity, the experience Allied commanders had gained in planning and achieving such a massive attack, and the integration of airborne, amphibious, and ground assets during the campaign meant that the invasion of Sicily was a resounding success. This experience would serve 1st Division well in the cauldron of the Normandy beachheads. *TRH/IWM*

commander, Major-General Allen, to take Niscemi and secure Ponte Olivo, thereby clearing the way to the high ground beyond Gela. The following day Ponte Olivo did indeed fall to Allen's men, who also inflicted further losses on the Livorno Division, and Niscemi fell on the 14th.

The breakout phase of the Allied invasion involved the 1st Infantry Division pushing northwest from Ponte Olivo toward the high ground running between Caltanissetta and Enna, and from there making for the northern coast, thereby cutting the island in two. The movement began on the 16th, with the division fighting off Group Ens of the German 15th Panzergrenadier Division. The River Salso to the east of Caltanissetta was crossed and a German attack beaten off at Gangi on 25 July. However, the division had to swing northeastward to conform with an attack by the British to the east rather than push directly on to the coast. Enna, in the centre of Sicily and formerly the headquarters of the Italian Sixth Army, fell. From there, the division took Petralia to the north and then headed east along Highway 120, which ran through the Caronie Mountains some 20 miles inland from the northern coast. The highway, running through Nicosia, Troina, Cesaro and Randazzo, was narrow and winding, full of steep gradients and sharp turns. Bridges and tunnels had been destroyed by the retreating Germans, who had also occupied the high ground that ran parallel to the route. Direct assault was impracticable, as Allen remarked: 'Had we kept up just a frontal attack, it would have meant just a bloody nose for us at every hill.' Slowly but surely, the division pushed the enemy off the high ground. By the end of July one intelligence officer reported: 'The Germans very tired, little ammo, many casualties, morale low.' The Germans withdrew from Nicosia on 27 July, allowing the division entry. Around 700 dispirited Italian troops were taken prisoner.

However, later events were to prove the intelligence officer wrong as the advancing Allied forces were only facing delaying parties, not the bulk of the German forces, most of which were positioned along and around the Etna Line. Troina was a key forward position of the line and heavily defended, although the US forces expected minimal resistance. On 31 July one of the division's regiments moved out from Nicosia toward Troina at dawn, which lay atop high cliffs some seven miles away. Early progress was as good as expected and the village of Cerami fell easily at 09.00 hours, but then the assault troops ran into stiffening German resistance.

On 1 August one of Allen's regimental commanders, Colonel John Bowen of the 26th, stated: 'I think there is a hell of a lot of stuff there up near our objective.' What had begun as a virtually bloodless push turned into a slogging match, with more and more of the division's strength committed. Air strikes were called in on the defenders, part of Major-General Eberhard Rodt's 15th Panzergrenadier Division, on 3 August, but the ground forces made little progress until the night of the 5th/6th, when the battered German defenders were given permission to abandon Troina to take up new positions on the Tortorici Line. By this stage all three of the 1st Division's infantry regiments, as well as two from Major-General Manton Eddy's newly arrived US 9th Division and a battalion of French Moroccan troops, had been committed to the fight for the hill-top village. Following the fall of Troina, the division was temporarily withdrawn from the front line and its responsibilities taken over by Eddy's command.

The belated capture of Troina did not satisfy Patton, who believed that both Allen and his second in command, General Theodore Roosevelt Jr., had not performed well enough during the battle. Bradley attempted to intervene stating that: 'General Allen can't be blamed for the setback. Troina is going to be tougher than we thought. The Kraut is as touchy as hell there.' This intervention was not enough and both Allen and Roosevelt were removed. Command of the 1st Division was given to Major General Clarence Huebner, a strict disciplinarian, who acted quickly to impose his will on the officers and men of the division. The division returned to action on the 12th, becoming involved in attempts to break through the Tortorici Line in the vicinity of Randazzo to the north of Mount Etna. By this stage of the campaign the Germans were undertaking a skilful withdrawal from the island, chiefly via Messina to the Italian mainland, but small delaying parties, booby-traps and the demolition of key points slowed the Allied advance. Nevertheless, Messina itself fell to the US 3rd Division on the 17th, signalling the completion of the 38-day campaign. The capture of Sicily ended the division's association with the Mediterranean theatre. It remained on the island during September and for much of October, but sailed for England on the 23rd to become part of the largest amphibious operation of all time – the D-Day invasion.

Below: Major General Clarence Huebner joined the 1st Division in 1910 as a private soldier. He subsequently served with the division in every rank from private to colonel. He became commanding general during the Sicily campaign. *US Army*

## OMAHA – THE GREATEST TEST

After arriving at Liverpool in the first week of November, the division moved south, establishing its headquarters at Blandford in Dorset. The various units were scattered about the county. For example, the 16th Infantry Regiment under Colonel George A. Taylor was based at Parnham House, near Beaminster, the 18th commanded by Colonel George Smith Jr. at Ilsington House at Puddletown, and Colonel John F. Seitz's 26th at Binnegar Hall, near Wareham. Over the following weeks the division would be brought up to strength with new replacements and begin the process of preparing for the invasion of Normandy, code-named

Operation 'Overlord'. The news that the division was to be one of the spearheads of the Normandy invasion did not initially go down well. Some felt that after North Africa and Sicily the division had done more than its share of the fighting and that the new divisions in the rapidly expanding US Army should take over. Even Bradley admitted that the decision to involve the 1st Division in a third amphibious assault caused him concern:

> 'Much as I dislike subjecting the 1st to still another landing, I felt that as a commander I had no other choice. My job was to get ashore, establish a lodgement, and destroy the Germans. In the accomplishment of that mission, there was little room for the nicities of justice. I felt compelled to employ the best troops I had, to minimise the risks and hoist the odds in our favour in any way that I could.'

## 1st Infantry Division in Dorset, England

Divisional strength as at 5 June 1944 — 34,142 men and 3,306 vehicles.

**Division HQ**
CO Maj-Gen Clarence R. Huebner
Div CP: Langton House, near Blandford Forum from 9 November 1943 till 2 June 1944, when the CP (Advanced) went on board USS *Ancon* and CP (Alternative) USS *Chase*.

**16th Infantry Regiment**
CO Col George A. Taylor
CP: Parnham House, near Beaminster. The infantry battalions, HQ Coy, Service Coy, Cannon Coy and A/tk Coy were in Bridport, Lyme Regis, Abbotsbury, Litton Cheney and Beaminster. They marshalled at Long Bredy before embarking.

**18th Infantry Regiment**
CO Col George A. Smith Jr
CP: Ilsington House, near Puddletown.
1st Bn: Piddlehinton Camp, moving on 12 January 1944 to Chickerell Camp.
2nd Bn and Cannon Coy: Broadmayne and West Knighton.
3rd Bn and Service Coy: Dorchester.
A/tk Coy: Winterborne St Martin.
HQ Coy: Puddletown

**26th Infantry Regiment**
CO Col John F. R. Seitz
CP: Binnegar Hall, near Wareham.
1st Bn, 2nd Bn, Cannon Coy and A/tk Coy: Swanage.
3rd Bn: Blandford.
Service Coy and HQ Coy: Wareham.

**1st Division Artillery**
CO Brig-Gen Clift Andrus
HQ and HQ Bty: Spettisbury.
Div Arty (5th, 7th, 32nd and 33rd Fd Arty Bns): Piddlehinton.

On 17 May 44, the HQ and HQ Baty left Spettisbury and was divided into four main groups: Command Group No 1 with Force O under CG Div Arty, CG No 2 with Force O under Div Arty S-3, D-Day transportation with Force O under Arty Survey, Remainder of battery with Force B under Bty Exec.

**1st Engineer Combat Battalion**
CO Lt-Col William B. Gara
HQ and Svc Coy (with Div HQ Coy A): Charmouth
Coy B: Corfe Castle
Coy C: Studland

**1st Division Signal Company**
CO: Maj Leonard T. Peters
Bryanston Camp, Blandford.

**1st Reconnaissance Troop**
CO: Capt William L. Blake
Initially at Norden Hill Camp, Maiden Newton, then in Piddlehinton Camp.

**1st Division MP Platoon**
CO: Maj Thomas F. Lancer
Initially all at Piddlehinton, then dispersed to Piddlehinton, Blandford, and Bournemouth.

**701st Ordnance Light Maintenance Company**
CO: Capt Raymond C. Huntoon
Dorchester

**1st Quartermaster Company**
CO: Capt John J. King
Dorchester.

**1st Medical Battalion**
CO: Lt-Col Samuel Bleichfield
Piddlehinton then to Cattistock on 12 January 1944

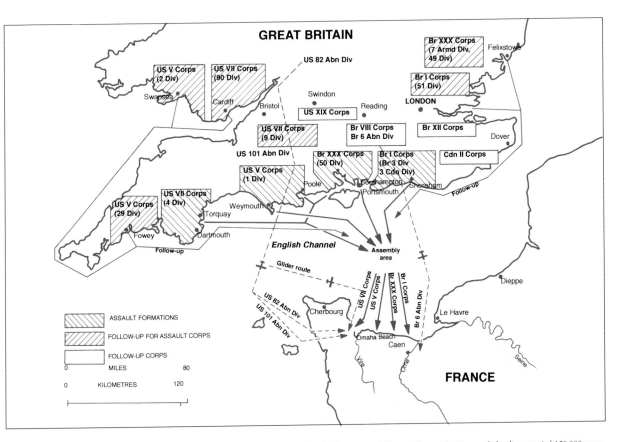

As the division settled in to its new billets in southwest England, the grumbling became less evident. Indeed, many took great pride in belonging to a unit that was considered absolutely vital to Operation 'Overlord'.

Between January and May 1944, elements of the 1st Division, along with other D-Day assault units, undertook a wide variety of training exercises, including spells at a camp established on the north Devon coast, which had been founded by US Lieutenant-Colonel Paul Thompson in September 1943. Here, and elsewhere, including at Slapton Sands, the troops learnt the techniques of amphibious assault under the most realistic possible conditions. Key to this was practising with the equipment needed to crack beach defences and establishing the tactics needed by the individual assault groups. These comprised some 31 men, the number that could be carried in the landing craft, who were equipped with a variety of suitable weapons for neutralising defensive positions, including bazookas, Bangalore torpedoes, flame-throwers and automatic weapons.

Each amphibious assault force was given the first letter of the code-name of the beach it was to attack. Force O, destined for Omaha Beach and including the 1st Infantry Division, began the embarkation process at the end of May, chiefly at the small ports of Poole, Portland and Weymouth. Yet few of those readying for D-Day knew that the precise date and hour of the invasion had yet to be fixed, and none realised the maelstrom into which they were to be thrown. Omaha was probably the most naturally strong defensive position of all of the five Allied invasion beaches on the Normandy coast. Stretching in a gentle curve for some four miles, each end was dominated by high ground – to the west lay the rocky outcrops of Pointe de la Percée in the west and Port-en-Bessin to the east. At low tide the firm sandy beach was some 300 to 400 yards wide, but at high tide it shrank greatly until just a few yards

Above: The Normandy landings carried 150,000 men from the south of England to the coast of northern France. This map shows the complex arrangements made to ensure that assembly, embarkation and departure were organised and protected. Some months earlier, off the Devon coast at Slapton Sands, E-boats got in amongst a D-Day training exercise, Exercise 'Tiger'. 1st Division was lucky not to be involved because 197 sailors and 441 US soldiers died as a result — more than would die on Utah beach — emphasising the need for secrecy, airpower and concentration of forces.

**Above:** With the background deleted by the censor to hide the location, this photograph shows US troops — probably from 1st Division — marching to an embarkation point. *TRH Pictures*

**Left:** The invasion begins — troops of 1st Infantry board landing craft. *George Forty collection*

**Opposite, Above:** Members of 1st Division's HQ Company eat their 'K' rations aboard a landing craft during Exercise 'Fabius' near Weymouth, England, 4 May 1944. *George Forty collection*

**Opposite, Below:** Men of the Company C, 1st Combat Engineer Battalion, 1st Infantry Division aboard an LCT awaiting departure for Normandy. *George Forty collection*

separated the Channel waters from what in 1944 was a bank of shingle up to nine feet high. Sections of the beach were also protected by a sea wall constructed from both wood and concrete. The beach was backed by a width of sometimes marshy ground, which in turn gave way to bluffs 100 feet high or more. Five exits from the beach, which would channel any attacking force, consisted of a number of steep sided narrow gullies. These were code-named D-1, D-3, E-1, E-3 and F-1 and were key objectives for troops trying to get off Omaha. Inland, the main settlement in the sparsely populated area was the village of Trevières, some four miles inland on the south bank of the River Aure. Closer to the beach, some 500 to 1,000 yards inland lay three villages running from west to east, Vierville-sur-Mer, St Laurent-sur-Mer and Colleville-sur-Mer. These were some 2,500 yards apart and were linked by a narrow coast road.

The naturally strong defences of Omaha had been greatly enhanced by extensive fortifications, many of which had been built or improved by the Todt Organisation at the express order of Field Marshal Erwin Rommel in the weeks before D-Day. At sea they were designed to stop any invasion force from getting ashore by destroying or damaging its amphibious craft during the run in to the beach or so disorganise any surviving forces (and their timetable) as to make any co-ordinated assault impossible. The defences began offshore with mines anchored in the English Channel and blocking the most likely routes to any potential invasion site. Next, thousands of obstacles had been concentrated between the high- and low-water marks running parallel to the shore and at various distances from it, either to rip the bottoms out of assault craft or smash them by explosive force. First, 'Belgian Gates', 10-foot high iron structures often topped by Teller land mines or artillery shells, were sited some 150 yards from the high-water mark. Next came tripod-like wooden structures, which had one longer beam angled toward the sea and lay 100 yards from the high-water line. These had also been fitted with mines. The densest line of obstacles was positioned some 70 yards from the shore. These consisted of six-foot lengths of steel rail, usually three or four sections, that had been welded at their centres so that they could not be tipped over easily. Known as Hedgehogs, these were designed to rip or tear the hull of an assault craft and channel the survivors into killing zones, as were similar pyramid-shaped devices, known as tetrahedra.

If the fixed defences offshore did not halt the invaders, they were to be held up on the beaches themselves by various natural and man-made defences and subjected to intense fire from small arms and heavier weapons. On Omaha itself, 12 concrete emplacements had been built to pour fire from artillery pieces along the beach. Next, came the positions that protected the five gullies that led inland from the beach. Successive lines of trenches had been dug on the slopes and these were manned by infantry with machine guns. Supporting these positions were small round concrete emplacements known as 'Tobruks' that held mortars or machine guns. All of these positions had been strengthened by extensive belts of barbed wire, minefields and anti-tank trenches. On the summit line of the bluffs lay eight larger concrete positions for artillery. Dummy positions had been built to dilute the impact of Allied supporting fire from offshore warships.

Typical of the defensive positions that faced the division at Omaha was Widerstandsnest 62 (Resistance Nest 62), which protected the beach sector designated Fox Green and the gully leading to Coleville-sur-Mer a mile inland. Extended and strengthened shortly before D-Day, W62 comprised reinforced-concrete gun emplacements, trenches and foxholes, all protected by barbed wire and mines. Aside from their personal weapons, the garrison, around 20 men, had charge

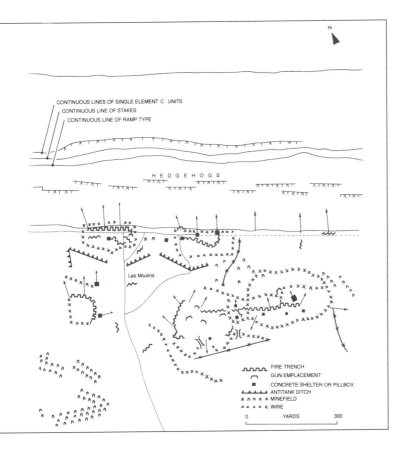

CONTINUOUS LINES OF SINGLE ELEMENT C UNITS
CONTINUOUS LINE OF STAKES
CONTINUOUS LINE OF RAMP TYPE

H E D G E H O G S

Les Moulins

FIRE TRENCH
GUN EMPLACEMENT
CONCRETE SHELTER OR PILLBOX
ANTITANK DITCH
MINEFIELD
WIRE

0        YARDS        300

**Left:** Defence in depth — the Atlantic Wall was not all concrete towers and emplacements, but it was nevertheless a substantial network of integrated defences. The Germans knew that they would have to destroy an invading force on the beaches: Allied airpower would make reinforcement difficult. So, the defences started with hedgehogs — mined metal stakes to stop landing craft making clear runs to the beach. In fact, these provided a small amount of shelter for the attacking troops on an otherwise murderous killing zone. A famous sequence of photographs by war photographer Robert Capa shows just that happening on Omaha. At the shoreline the fire trenches started, with gun emplacements at key points, minefields, wire, anti-tank ditches and concrete emplacements. These emplacements and guns were not, however, all facing the front; subtly sited to allow maximum use of enfilading fire along the beaches, they made difficult targets for offshore bombardment. Indeed, the bombardment of German positions on Omaha beach was not nearly as effective as expected and most of the 60 artillery pieces and 85 machine guns were still operational when V Corps' forces landed. This drawing shows the defences around Draw 3 between *Widerstandsnest* 66 (on the right of the draw) and WN68. It was up this draw that 29th Division troops broke through German lines and reached the top of the bluff behind the beach.

of two Czech 75mm field guns, a 50mm anti-tank gun, a 50mm mortar, two light machine guns, and a pair of Polish heavy machine guns. An artillery spotter was on hand to call down fire from a battery of 105mm self-propelled guns positioned inland that had been given prearranged targets on the beach. Finally, Allied intelligence had miscalculated the calibre of the defenders, stating that Omaha was held by a single battalion, some 800 men, of the low-grade 716th Infantry Division, which consisted of Poles and Russians. In reality, the enemy positions were manned by three battalions of General Dietrich Kraiss's 352nd Infantry Division, which was of generally better quality and had recently conducted rigorous anti-invasion exercises.

Allied planners had divided Omaha into eight sectors, which varied in length from around 500 yards to more than 1,800. The troops committed to the landings were drawn from the US V Corps under General Leonard Gerow, itself part of General Omar Bradley's US First Army. Of the first wave, elements of the 29th Infantry Division's 116th Infantry Regiment were tasked with assaulting the western half of Omaha, landing on sectors code-named Charlie, Dog Green, Dog White, Dog Red and Easy Green. The leading elements of the 1st Division's assault were drawn from the 16th Regiment under Colonel George Taylor, which was to come ashore at the beach sectors to the east known as Easy Red, Fox Green and Fox Red. The objectives of these troops and the follow-on forces at Omaha on 6 June were to cut through the beach defences, push inland beyond the three coastal villages and establish a perimeter along the line of the main coast road running between Isigny and Bayeux to the north of Trevières, thereby linking up with the British forces that were to land at Gold Beach to the east. By the end of D-Day some 40,000 men and 3,500

French Croix de Guerre with Palm, Streamer embroidered Normandy

HQ and HQ Company, 1st Infantry Division
HQ and HQ Battery, 1st Infantry Division Artillery
announced in Department of the Army General Orders 43, 1950 (along with other attached units):

An elite unit which landed on the beaches of Colleville, 6 June 1944, in spite of stubborn resistance of the coastal fortifications and of the enemy reinforcements. In the afternoon of the same day it seized the crest overhanging the beaches and, pushing toward the interior, occupied strategic positions in spite of the furious German counterattacks. In spite of its heavy losses, it succeeded in establishing and consolidating a strong bridgehead, thus contributing to the decisive victory of Normandy.

vehicles of all types were to have been landed at Omaha, a staggering amount of traffic. However, these were ambitious plans that demanded complete adherence to a complex timetable that could so easily be disrupted. H-Hour at Omaha was set for 06.30, some 60 minutes after both dawn and the lowest tide point, and the beach and routes through the bluffs were to be cleared by H+2 – 08.30 hours.

The first wave of assault ships, mostly Landing Craft, Tank, reached their final forming up point 12 miles off Omaha at around 04.00 and 70 minutes later began moving to final positions, which lay some three miles offshore. Behind them the infantry scrambled down the nets lowered over the sides of the larger assault vessels and 30 at a time took their (standing) positions in the notoriously unseaworthy Higgins boats. Matters began to go wrong on Omaha even before the leading assault infantry had touched solid land. First, the preliminary air bombardment had largely missed its targets on the beach, with many bombs falling harmlessly inland, due to dense cloud cover over Omaha. Second, supporting naval fire on the beaches, which had begun at around 05.30, was halted or switched inland around 50 minutes later for fear of hitting friendly forces in the smoke, although many of the enemy emplacements had survived the short barrage with little damage. None of the 20 man garrison at W62, for example, was killed or injured during this time. Equally, the following drenching of the beaches by 14 Landing Craft, Tank (Rocket) with 14,000 missiles in little more than a minute, while mightily impressive to onlookers, had negligible impact on the defenders. Many of the amphibious Duplex Drive (DD) Sherman tanks, which were supposed to land slightly ahead of the infantry to suppress enemy fire, had been swamped in the Channel. Most had been offloaded far too far from the shore and quickly foundered in the rough water whipped up by 10–18 knot northwesterly winds that smashed the flimsy canvas 'skirts' that supposedly gave the DD tanks buoyancy. Others were lost when the LCT carrying them hit submerged mines or were smashed by German artillery. Of the 29 earmarked for Easy Red, 21 were swamped on the run in, one was sunk by a landing craft, and two were destroyed in the shallows by German fire.

**Right:** An LCI packed with troops en route to France.
*TRH/US Navy*

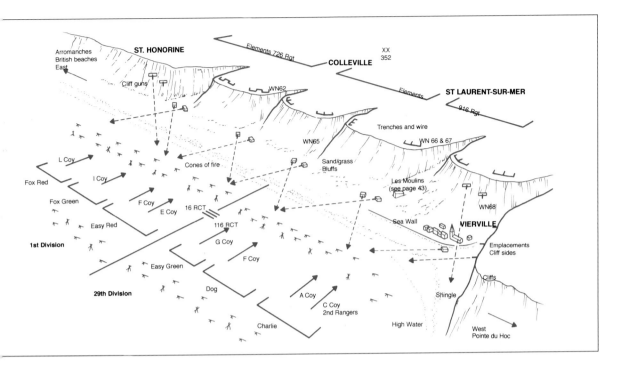

Above: The US V Corps beaches were divided into two Regimental Combat Teams — the 16th (1st Division) and the 116th (29th Division). 1st Division's were Easy Red, Fox Green and Fox Red opposite Coleville; 29th Division's were Easy Green, Dog and Charlie opposite St Laurent-sur-Mer. The defenders were elements of the 726th and 916th Regiments of the German 352nd Division. Their excellent positions made 'Omaha' the toughest of all the Allied invasion points.

The outcome of all these factors was that the defenders were alert, mostly unscathed and holding virtually intact positions as the assault infantry headed for the beach. They had expected to come ashore and fight their way inland against smashed defences and their few remaining demoralised defenders while being supported by the tanks and armoured bulldozers that would quickly create paths through the German defences; instead they would be virtually alone. As planned two battalions of the 1st Division's 16th Regiment, the 2nd and 3rd, landed in the first wave, although with little support from the DD tanks. The job of the their assault teams, usually platoons of 30 men, was to deal with pre-designated points of enemy resistance, while demolition teams cleared the beach defences to ease the way for the following waves. However, rough seas, the turning tide, confusion and enemy fire resulted in many of the first (and later) companies landing at the wrong point.

As the Higgins boats touched bottom (many landing craft had already stuck on hidden sandbars), many were hit and the assault troops walked into a hail of enemy fire from front and flank as they struggled through the shallows and across the sand or the shingle bank or took cover behind beach obstacles. Casualties were heavy, particularly among junior officers. Some men hurried to the comparative safety of the shingle bank; others huddled as best they could among the German sea defences; others, often acting on their own initiative, slowly fought their way off the murderous beach. As a few small, scattered groups made their way up the bluffs, many others remained pinned down behind the shingle bank. At around 08.00 the 16th Regiment's commander, 47-year-old George Taylor came ashore and made his way to the bank. Surveying the leaderless troops around him amid the enemy fire, he galvanised nearby groups with a few words: 'There are only two kinds of people on this beach: the dead and those about to die. So let's get the hell out of here.'

The men moved gradually forward. Bangalore torpedoes were used to blow gaps in the barbed wire, paths were cleared through the minefields and marked, and flame-throwers and satchel charges were used to neutralise pillboxes. Slowly but surely, the defences between the beach and the bluffs and gullies were breached, but

## D-Day casualties

|  | KIA | MIA | Wounded | Total |
|---|---|---|---|---|
| 1st Div | 124 | 431 | 1,083 | 1,638 |
| 29th Div | 280 | 896 | 1,027 | 2,203 |
| Total | 552 | 1,896 | 2,766 | 5,214 |

the ways inland from the beaches were still mostly blocked. To make matters wors
the tide was coming in, thereby shrinking the already congested beach, yet mo
and more equipment was heading for shore. To Bradley at his command post on th
USS *Augusta*, Omaha appeared an ongoing disaster. With no exits from the beac
available, he briefly contemplated sending the follow-on waves elsewhere.

At 09.50, Huebner ordered the division's 18th Infantry Regiment to assault Ea
Beach, the western edge of which was the dividing line between the sectors give
to the 1st and 29th Divisions. The largest of the sectors, Easy Red, quickly becam
congested. By 10.00, the tide was almost at its highest mark, thereby narrowing th
beach and hiding many of the offshore defences. Also, the 29th Division's 115
Infantry Regiment, actually assigned to Dog Red, began landing on Easy Red
10.30. By this stage troops were moving up the bluffs between the gulli
designated E-1 and E-3. It did not seem much, but advances like this and elsewhe
were slowly paving the way for the move inland. Others followed to the top of th
bluffs and edged their way inland. The fighting against fierce German resistance w
often at close range as the already exhausted troops edged along narrow roa
flanked by thick hedges toward their objectives.

By the end of the day, the Omaha beachhead was little more than 1,500 yar
deep at its greatest extent and some six miles long, far less than had been planne
and there was no continuous perimeter. Weary groups of soldiers simply establishe
positions, some 18 dotted around the three inland villages, where they coul
Behind them the beach was still under occasional fire, but there was no doubtin
that the Atlantic Wall had been irrevocably breached. This victory had been won
a high cost – some 2,400 troops were killed, wounded or missing at Omah
compared with around a dozen killed during the US VI Corps' landings at Utah Beac
to the west. For the Allied command, the next tasks were to expand and unite th
various beachheads to provide room for the arrival of further Allied forces and the
begin the breakout from Normandy and the liberation of France. For its part, th
German high command was rushing fresh troops to the theatre, many of the
veterans of the Eastern Front.

## THE NORMANDY BREAKOUT

The task facing the division during the breakout phase of the campaign was mad
more difficult by the nature of the Normandy countryside – the bocage. This was
patchwork of small fields and narrow roads separated by ditches and dense hedge

Right: Landing diagram for Omaha Easy Green and
Dog beaches (those on which 29th Division landed).
In the diagram the lozenges are amphibious (DD =
Duplex Drive) tanks; the other vessels being:
I = LCI = Landing craft infantry
M = LCM = Landing craft mechanised
T = LCT = Landing craft tank
A = LCA = Landing craft assault
V = LCVP = Landing craft vehicle and personnel
D = DUKW amphibious vehicles

## MEN AND EQUIPMENT OF A TYPICAL INFANTRY REGIMENT AND BATTALION IN 1944

| REGIMENT T/07-11 (26 FEB 44) | | | | | |
|---|---|---|---|---|---|
| Officers | 152 | Carbine, .30-cal | 836 | Machine gun, .50-cal | 6 |
| Warrant Officers | 5 | Rifle, .30-cal | 1,990 | Machine gun, .30-cal Heavy | 8 |
| Enlisted Men | 3,100 | Pistol, .45-cal | 293 | Machine gun, .30-cal Light | 6 |
| 105mm Howitzer | 6 | Truck, 2½-ton | 34 | Mortar, 81mm | 6 |
| 57mm Gun | 18 | Truck, 1½-ton or 1-ton | 31 | Mortar, 60mm | 9 |
| Machine gun, .50-cal | 35 | Truck, ¾-ton | 12 | Rocket Launcher, 2.36in A/tk | 29 |
| Machine gun, .30-cal Heavy | 24 | Truck, ¼-ton | 149 | Carbine, .30-cal | 219 |
| Machine gun, .30-cal Light | 18 | | | Rifle, .30-cal | 571 |
| Mortar, 81mm | 18 | BATTALION T/07-15 (26 FEB 44) | | Pistol, .45-cal | 81 |
| Mortar, 60mm | 37 | Officers | 35 | Truck, 1½-ton or 1-ton | 4 |
| Rocket Launcher, 2.36in A/tk | 112 | Enlisted Men | 836 | Truck, ¾-ton | 2 |
| | | 57mm Gun | 3 | Truck, ¼-ton | 34 |

# LANDING DIAGRAM, OMAHA BEACH

## (SECTOR OF 116th RCT)

| | EASY GREEN | DOG RED | DOG WHITE | DOG GREEN |
|---|---|---|---|---|
| H - 5 | | | ◊◊◊◊ ◊◊◊◊ ◊◊◊◊ ◊◊◊◊<br>Co C (DD)  743 Tk Bn | ◊◊◊◊ ◊◊◊◊ ◊◊◊◊ ◊◊◊◊<br>Co B (DD)  743 Tk Bn |
| H-HOUR | T T T T<br>Co A 743 Tk Bn | T T T T<br>Co A 743 Tk Bn | | |
| H+01 | V V V V V V<br>Co E 116 Inf | V V V V V V<br>Co F 116 Inf | V V V V V V<br>Co G  116 Inf | A A A A A A<br>Co A 116 Inf |
| H+03 | M M M<br>146 Engr CT | M M M<br>146 Engr CT | M M<br>146 Engr CT | M M M<br>146 Engr CT | Demolitions<br>Control Boat | A A<br>Co C<br>2d Ranger Bn |
| H+30 | V V V V V<br>Co H, HQ Co E Co H<br>AAAW Btry    116 Inf    AAAW Btry | HQ HQ HQ Co<br>V V V V V V<br>2d Bn  CoH CoF CoH 2d Bn<br>116 Inf        AAAW Btry | V V V V V<br>Co H HQ Co G Co H<br>AAAW Btry    116 Inf    AAAW Btry | A A A A A A A A V<br>Co B  HQ Co A  Co B<br>116 Inf        AAAW Btry |
| H+40 | M<br>M<br>112 Engr Bn | 112 Engr<br>V V V V M<br>Co D 81 Cml Wpns Bn  149 Engr<br>Beach Bn | V M<br>149 Engr  121 Engr Bn<br>Beach Bn | HQ<br>A A A A M V V V V V<br>1st Bn 116        Co D 116 Inf<br>149 Beach Bn 121 Engr |
| H+50 | V V V V V V V<br>Co L 116 Inf | V V V V V V V<br>Co I 116 Inf | V V V V V V<br>Co K 116 Inf | M V V V V V V V<br>121 Engr     Co C 116 Inf<br>Bn |
| H+57 | | V V V V V V V V V<br>HQ Co 3d Bn      Co M 116 Inf | | V V V V<br>Co B 81 Cml Wpns Bn |
| H+60 | T | V T T T T<br>112 Engr<br>Bn | V<br>HQ & HQ Co 116 Inf | T T T A A A A A<br>121 Engr Bn    Co A & B<br>2d Ranger Bn |
| H+65 | | | | A A A A A A A<br>5th Ranger Bn |
| H+70 | I<br>149 Engr Beach Bn | I<br>112 Engr Bn | I<br>Alt HQ & HQ Co 116 Inf | M T T A A A A A A A<br>121 Engr Bn      5th Ranger Bn |
| H+90 | | | T T T T T<br>58 FA Bn Armd | |
| H+100 | | | I<br>6th Engr Sp Brig | |
| H+110 | D D D D  D D D D  D D D D D<br>111 FA Bn (3 Btrys in DUKWS) | D D D  D D D D<br>AT Plat 2d Bn  AT Plat 3d Bn<br>29 Sig Bn | | D D D  D D D D D D<br>AT Plat    Cn Co 116 Inf<br>1st Bn |
| H+120 | T T T<br>AT Co 116 Inf<br>467 AAAW Bn    467 AAAW Bn | T T T T T<br>467 AAW Bn  149  Engr<br>AT Co 116 Inf      Beach Bn | T T<br>467 AAAW Bn | T T<br>467 AAAW Bn |
| H+150 | | DD Tanks | I<br>HQ Co 116 Inf<br>104 Med Bn | |
| H+180<br>to<br>H+215 | T T | T  T  T<br>D D D D D D D D D D D<br>461 Amphibious Truck Co | M T M T M T<br>Navy Salvage | T T T T T T |
| H+225 | D D D D D D D D D D D D D D D<br>461 Amph Trk Co | T | T T | |

| | | | | |
|---|---|---|---|---|
| I LCI | M LCM | A LCA | ◊ DD Tank | Note: Plan as of 11th May |
| | T LCT | V LCVP | D DUKW | |

**Opposite, Above:** Follow-up troops come ashore on 7 June. *TRH/US Army*

**Opposite, Below:** Later troop landings come into Omaha. In the background, M3 halftracks towing 57mm anti-tank guns make their way along the beach. In the distance a line of troops wends its way up the bluff behind the beach. *TRH/US Army*

**Above:** DUKWs coming in to Omaha. *TRH/US Army*

**Left:** Follow-up troops wading on to the beaches. *TRH/IWM*

**Below left:** German soldier treated by US medic, on Omaha at Colleville. *TRH/US Army*

growing out of thick earth banks. Small scattered villages and woods also provided excellent cover for enemy forces and made ideal strongpoints. Although the forces opposing the Allies were initially small, they were well motivated and highly adept. Equally, as much of the fighting would be at close range because of the terrain, two of the Allied trump cards – support from ground-attack aircraft and warships offshore – would be somewhat restricted. Equally, the Allied numerical superiority in tanks would count for little in such terrain as they could not be manoeuvred easily; Normandy would become a close-quarters slogging match for the front-line combat infantry. However, the opening phase of the division's breakout from Omaha proved to be relatively easy in the face of only scattered German opposition.

The first stage was completed within 48 hours, when elements of the 1st Division pushed eastward toward Port-en-Bessin, where a link-up was made on the 8th with British forces that had been pushing westward out of Gold Beach. While this was taking place other of the division's units were able to push south over the Aure River to deepen the Allied lodgement. The 16th Infantry Regiment reached the vital east–west highway running from Bayeux to St Lô on the 10th. From this position the advance continued south, crossing the Drôme River and pushing beyond the village of Balleroy toward Caumont, which fell to the 18th and 26th Infantry Regiments on 13 June. The capture of Caumont marked the end of the division's part in the first stage of the battle for Normandy. It was temporarily withdrawn from the front line, where it was replaced by the US 5th Infantry Division, and sent to rest and recuperate at Colombières, a small village just a few miles inland from Omaha. The cost of the few days ashore in Normandy had been high. During the week from D-Day to the fall of Caumont the division recorded 1,744 casualties.

The Allied strategy to break out from Normandy in the days after the D-Day landings became stuck at Caen, where the British and Canadians were battering away to little effect against a skilful German defence. Their attacks were drawing in more and more of the German reinforcements arriving in Normandy, thereby lessening the forces faced by the US forces to the west, but it became increasingly apparent that any breakout into the 'good' tank country beyond the Normandy bocage would have to come from elsewhere. The solution to the stalemate lay with Bradley's First Army. Since D-Day his forces had linked up Omaha and Utah beaches and, while the Anglo-Canadian

**Below:** The US First Army explodes through the German defences in Operation 'Cobra' — the breakout from the Normandy bridgehead. It was the end of any idea the Germans may have had about rolling the invaders back into the sea. After heavy fighting the Germans would retreat through the Falaise pocket and the Allies would liberate France. 1st Division played a major role in the operation in spite of over 1,700 casualties since 6 June.

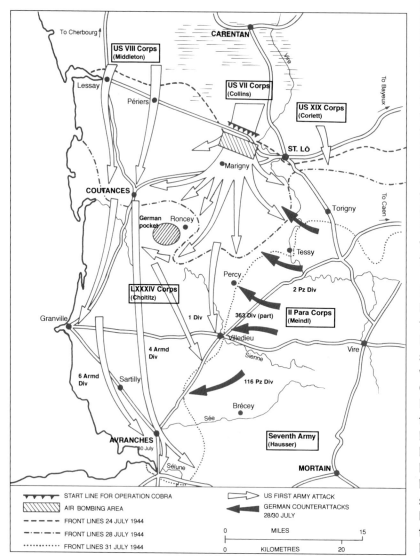

forces had been battling at Caen, had liberated the Cherbourg Peninsula by the end of June and advanced southward to hold a line running from St Lô to Lessay on the Atlantic coast by latter part of July. Bradley's plan, code-named Operation 'Cobra', envisaged a concentrated punch through the German defences close to St Lô, followed by an armoured exploitation of the rupture. The attack was to be preceded by a massive air bombardment. Briefing his subordinates Bradley stated that the fighting would be hard and heavy casualties were to be expected but there was little alternative if the deadlock was to be broken. He concluded: 'This thing must be bold.' The operation was originally scheduled to open on 20 July but bad weather brought a succession of delays. Bradley's mood did not improve when a number of Allied bombers mistakenly carried out a raid on the 24th. Apart from possibly alerting the Germans to 'Cobra', some of the bombing fell short, killing 25 US soldiers and wounding a further 131.

Above: Bradley with Montgomery and Dempsey. *TRH Pictures*

Operation 'Cobra' finally began on the 25th, but once again the preceding air attack, which included more than 1,500 Flying Fortress and Liberator bombers, partly fell on the US assault troops. Some 490 men were wounded and 111 killed, including Lieutenant-General Lesley McNair, the commander of the US Army Ground Forces and a former officer of the 1st Infantry Division, who was visiting the front. However, this setback was nothing compared to the damage inflicted on some of the German defenders. The bombers had concentrated on a four-mile long sector of the front immediately to the northwest of St Lô held by the crack Panzer Lehr Division, whose commander, Lieutenant-General Fritz Bayerlein, remarked: 'My front line looked like a lunar landscape and at least 70 percent of my troops were out of action – dead, wounded, crazed or numb.' Elements of General J. Lawton Collins' US VII Corps of Bradley's First Army poured through this gap, spearheaded by armour, thereby opening a defended corridor between the villages of Marigny and St Gilles through which other units would drive. The 1st Infantry Division, motorised for this stage of the operation, was to be part of this follow-on force. Accompanied by part of the US 3rd Armored Division, it was to push south and then east toward the town of Coutances by way of Marigny.

In reality, the bombers had not wholly obliterated the German defenders and the first day saw the US forces gain little ground. Shortly after daybreak on the 26th the 1st Division was committed to the attack and began to advance on the village of Marigny. The advance proved difficult. Despite aid from ground-attack aircraft, tanks and massed artillery, the division ran into fierce resistance from scattered pockets of the German 353rd Infantry Division and the formidable 2nd SS Panzer Division. Two days of heavy fighting found the 1st Division still one mile short of its target. Nevertheless, 'Cobra' was succeeding and the Germans facing the 1st Division had to pull back due to successes elsewhere or face encirclement. As they did so the German defences collapsed, opening the possibilities of a major Allied breakout into Brittany and also eastward toward Paris. US units pushed rapidly southward. After taking Marigny, the 1st Division drove south parallel to the coast, securing crossings over the Sée River to the east of Avranches on the 31st and then moved southeastward toward Mortain. 'Cobra' was a major success and offered a clear chance to end the stalemate in Normandy. In the last six days of July, the US 1st Army had taken 20,000 prisoners, while Collins' VII Corps had advanced more than 35 miles. All this was a far cry from the dispiriting stop-start progress in the weeks immediately after D-Day.

The rapid advance of the US forces to the south and east during Operation 'Cobra' was partly matched by Anglo-Canadian attacks through and south of Caen. Together, they offered the tantalising prospect of surrounding the German Seventh Army under General Paul Hausser. Hausser's force, along with the Fifth Panzer Army under General Hans Eberbach, comprised the greater part of the German Army Group B under Field Marshal Günther von Kluge, and it should have been withdrawn to a less exposed position. Many senior German commanders, including von Kluge, advocated such a strategy following 'Cobra', but Adolf Hitler refused their request and ordered a counterattack, Operation 'Luttich', that was to drive through Mortain in the direction of Avranches. The 1st Division, which had its headquarters in the vicinity of Juvigny-le-Tertre by the first week of August, would have faced the SS-led spearhead of the German attack but was in fact withdrawn from the line on 6th August. Its replacement, the US 30th Infantry Division, played a distinguished role in defeating 'Luttich', which opened the following day and was effectively defeated within 48 hours.

By the second week of August the Allied plan to entrap the German Seventh Army was moving ahead. To the north the Anglo-Canadian forces were pushing southward toward Falaise in the face of stubborn resistance, while General George Patton's recently activated US Third Army to the south, was making a wide swinging manoeuvre northward in the direction of Argentan following the exploitation of the 'Cobra' offensive. The US VII Corps, which included the 1st Division, was moving on a roughly parallel course to Patton's forces but a little to the north. Accompanied by the US 3rd Armored Division it looped south of Mortain in the direction of Mayenne and then drove north towards the villages of Bagnoles-de-l'Orne and La-Ferté-Macé, which lay on the southwest perimeter of what became known as the Falaise Pocket. However, due to German resistance and Allied misunderstandings the pocket was only slowly

Below: Infantrymen show fatigue as they grab a quick smoke after six days' intensive fighting. *TRH/US Army*

sealed. It was not until 22nd August that the fighting ended.

Although some German forces had escaped, the scale of the Allied victory was nevertheless impressive. The German Seventh and Fifth Panzer Armies had virtually ceased to exist – some 50,000 men had been captured and an estimated 10,000 killed. Huge quantities of equipment had also been destroyed or abandoned. The scenes in the pocket were horrendous not least due to the devastation wrought on the Germans by Allied ground-attack aircraft. The US First Army's operations report noted: 'The roads and fields were littered with thousands of enemy dead and wounded, wrecked and burning vehicles, smashed artillery pieces, cars laden with the loot of France overturned and smouldering, dead horses and cattle swelling in the summer's heat.' Equally importantly, the long slogging match through the bocage country of Normandy was over and the road to Paris and the German frontier beyond was open. Facing little resistance in the aftermath of the German debacle at Falaise, US forces had already established a secure bridgehead over the Seine River on the 20th and Paris itself was liberated five days later.

Above: After the beaches came the bocage. These infantrymen, one with a carbine, one with a rifle, have removed their packs to advance to contact. *TRH/National Archives*

# THE ALLIED ADVANCE TO THE RHINE

With Germany's Army Group B, now commanded by Field Marshal Walther Model, in disarray, the Allied supreme commander, General Dwight D. Eisenhower, proposed a broad-front drive across eastern France toward the River Rhine and the German frontier, despite concerns over the growing exhaustion of the Allied troops and their ever-lengthening supply lines. The US First Army, now commanded by General Courtney Hodges as Bradley had been promoted to take command of the new US 12th Army Group, and containing the 1st Division, was to strike northeastward from around Paris, with the aim of cutting off the line of retreat of any German forces operating in northern France and also preventing them from establishing a defensive line along the River Meuse. The operation began on 26 August and progress was rapid in the face of mostly negligible enemy resistance. For the troops who had battled slowly through Normandy it was an exhilarating period of rapid movement. By the 30th the division had reached Soissons on the River Aisne some 50 miles from Paris and was then ordered almost directly northward toward the Belgian town of Mons as part of a plan to prevent the escape of German troops from northeast France. In early September, the remnants of several German units were virtually annihilated in the Mons Pocket. The 1st Division played a key part in a battle that one witness described as 'like shooting sitting pigeons'. Its role was cited in an order of the day of the Belgian Army, which read:

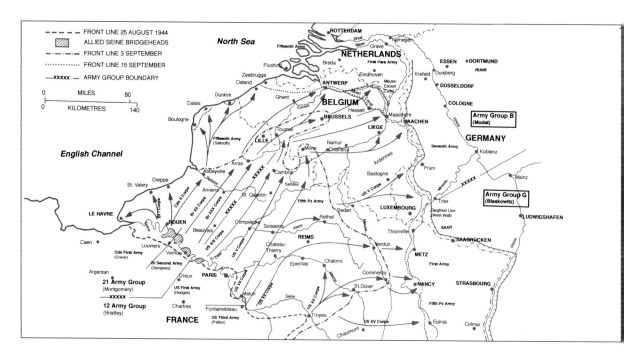

**Above:** After crossing the Seine in late August the Allies advanced towards Germany, British and Canadians to the north, United States' forces to the south. This map shows the front lines between 25 August and 15 September.

'From 3 to 5 September 1944, the division and the attached units in the area of Mons, under heavy pressure, destroyed an enemy pocket, including approximately 9,000 men of the 348th Infantry Division of the 18th German Air Army, and of the 6th Parachute Division. During this operation, the 1st Infantry Division of the United States Army and the attached units, after valiant efforts, captured more than 5,000 prisoners, killed or wounded 4,000 soldiers, and captured or destroyed more than 1,500 vehicles and 40 tanks. The division also took the commanding officer of the 6th German Airborne Division prisoner.'

After Mons, the division continued its advance across central Belgium passing close to Namur on 7 September, reaching the old fortress town of Liège two days later and then pushing toward the German frontier city of Aachen, which lay within the defences of the Siegfried Line. It was here along the border that German resistance stiffened in part due to the energetic work of the commander-in-chief in the west, Field Marshal Gerd von Rundstedt, who saw that the fall of the city to the Allies would open the way to Cologne and the Ruhr industrial area. It had to be defended at all costs. The battle for Aachen opened on the 12th with the division launching an attack against the city's municipal forest that met heavy resistance. Little progress was made for the remainder of the month and during the first week of October in part due to the growing supply shortages that hamstrung operations by Bradley's 12th Army Group.

The attack was renewed on 8 October, when a massive artillery and air bombardment heralded the opening phase. The First Army's XIX Corps under Major-General Charles Corlett attacked on a five-mile front, but so fierce was the resistance that his forces advanced little more than five miles in five days. However, this was enough to allow the US VII Corps under Collins to push southeast and complete the encirclement of the town on the 10th. As part of Collins' corps, the 1st Division was heavily engaged. On the 8th the 18th Infantry Regiment was pushing through

Verlautenheide, the 26th Infantry Regiment was making for the city centre, and the 16th Infantry Regiment was holding defensive positions near Eilendorf. Between the 12th and 15th, the 26th battled its way through a zone of factories between Aachen and Haaren, and was able to capture the greater part of Observatory Hill. The US attacks were renewed on the 18th, which completed the capture of Observatory Hill and forced the Germans to retire into the town's western suburbs. Intense street fighting followed and it was only on the 21st that the remaining 4,000 German defenders surrendered.

The division's place in the line at Aachen was taken over by the US 104th Division and it prepared for the next phase of the drive into Germany involving the US First Army – the battle to secure crossing points on the Roer River to the east of Aachen. This attack opened on 16 November, but progress was painfully slow. The 16th Infantry Regiment was able to capture Laufenburg Castle on the 20th but had to fight hard against a German counterattack at Merode nine days later. By the end of the month the division had been able to push the line forward no more than five miles. It was clear that the Roer crossing would have to be postponed. Exhausted by the battles at Aachen and the Roer, the greater part of the division was pulled back for rest on 5 December and its positions taken over by the US 9th Infantry Division. Within two weeks, however, it would be battling to defeat the last great German offensive in the west, Operation 'Wacht am Rhein' – the Battle of the Bulge.

The Battle of the Bulge was Hitler's last gamble against the western Allies. At his bidding, the best remaining German forces not facing the Russians, as well as second rate units, gathered in great secret in the wooded Ardennes. They intended to attack in overwhelming strength a weak sector of the Allied line held by the US VIII Corps, punch a hole through it to separate the American and British armies, and then swing northward to seize the port of Antwerp. The storm broke along a 80-mile front between Monschau and Echternach at 05.30 hours on 16 December 1944. Essential to the German plan was the protection of the northern and southern flanks of their line of advance. In the north this task was entrusted to the Sixth SS Panzer Army under SS General Josef 'Sepp' Dietrich, but the advance was delayed by the US 99th Infantry Division and its heavy artillery support. Although in the centre German troops had made excellent progress, despite stubborn resistance from pockets of US forces, the future of the offensive increasingly lay with the need to secure the flanks of the advance. If this did not occur then the Allies would surely counterattack through them. For the Germans speed was of the essence but delaying actions, like those of the 99th and, most memorably, the US 101st Airborne Division around Bastogne and the US 7th Armored Division at St Vith, were denying them the time and room to capitalise on any gains they had made.

The 1st Division was one of those Allied units flung into the battle along the northern shoulder of the Bulge. The plan was to drive into the Bulge from north and south with the aim of linking up near the village of Houffalize. One of the key positions in the northern shoulder was Elsenborn Ridge in the vicinity of Malmédy. Between the 21st and 28th, the division defended this vital position as a prelude to the Allied counterattack, and in the first days of January 1945, a time of bitter winter weather, the Allies in the north rolled forward. On the 15th the division took Steinbach, thereby opening the way for the US 7th Armored division to push on to St Vith. Step by step the Bulge was being eliminated. Among the actions fought by the 1st Division were a stiff battle around Schoppen and the clearance of the Bambusch Woods. By the end of the month the battle was over; Hitler's great gamble had failed. US forces were back on the Siegfried Line. The 1st Division's place at the front was taken over by the 99th Infantry Division on 5 February.

Cited in the Order of the Day of the Belgian Army for action at Eupen-Malmédy

HQ and HQ Company, 1st Infantry Division
HQ and HQ Battery, 1st Infantry Division Artillery
announced in Department of the Army General Orders 43, 19 December 1950 (along with other attached units):

The Division fought against the enemy in the northern flank of the German counteroffensive in the Ardennes in the area of Eupen-Malmédy. These counterattacks were launched by the enemy on 28 and 30 December, 1944, but they were repulsed after heavy combat. This action prevented the expansion of the critical break-through. Independently of the strenuous defense, a strong base was established that later formed the pivot of attacks against western penetrations of the enemy. After the enemy counter-attacks were efficiently stopped, the 1st Infantry Division of the US Army and the attached units pushed forward to reduce the pockets and throw the enemy out of Belgian territory.

Following this temporary respite, it shortly returned to action, taking over from the US 8th Infantry Division for the second attempt to cross the Roer, south of the river's dams. For this mission it was assigned to Major-General John Millikin's US II Corps. The operation opened on the 23rd and two days later the 16th Infantry Regiment crossed the river at Kreuznau. Burg fell to the division two days later and the obstacle of the Neffel River was breached on 1st March. It was clear that German resistance west of the Rhine River was crumbling fast, a fact reinforced when the division captured Bonn on its west bank on the 9th after two days of combat.

# FROM THE RHINE TO VICTORY

In mid-March the division began to move across the Rhine to exploit the bridgehead on its east bank that had developed following the recent capture of the intact bridge at Remagen. In the face of little opposition units of the US First Army moved forward some 45 miles in just two days. Pushing toward the Sieg River in the direction of

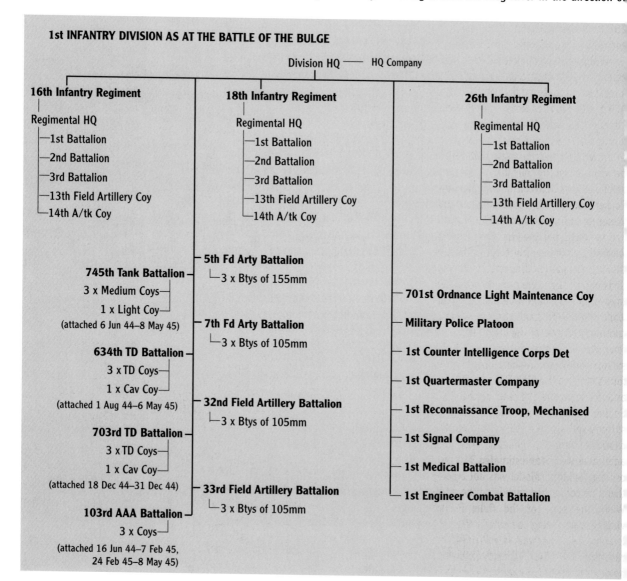

**1st INFANTRY DIVISION AS AT THE BATTLE OF THE BULGE**

Division HQ — HQ Company

**16th Infantry Regiment**

Regimental HQ
- 1st Battalion
- 2nd Battalion
- 3rd Battalion
- 13th Field Artillery Coy
- 14th A/tk Coy

**745th Tank Battalion**
3 x Medium Coys
1 x Light Coy
(attached 6 Jun 44–8 May 45)

**634th TD Battalion**
3 x TD Coys
1 x Cav Coy
(attached 1 Aug 44–6 May 45)

**703rd TD Battalion**
3 x TD Coys
1 x Cav Coy
(attached 18 Dec 44–31 Dec 44)

**103rd AAA Battalion**
3 x Coys
(attached 16 Jun 44–7 Feb 45,
24 Feb 45–8 May 45)

**18th Infantry Regiment**

Regimental HQ
- 1st Battalion
- 2nd Battalion
- 3rd Battalion
- 13th Field Artillery Coy
- 14th A/tk Coy

**5th Fd Arty Battalion**
3 x Btys of 155mm

**7th Fd Arty Battalion**
3 x Btys of 105mm

**32nd Field Artillery Battalion**
3 x Btys of 105mm

**33rd Field Artillery Battalion**
3 x Btys of 105mm

**26th Infantry Regiment**

Regimental HQ
- 1st Battalion
- 2nd Battalion
- 3rd Battalion
- 13th Field Artillery Coy
- 14th A/tk Coy

**701st Ordnance Light Maintenance Coy**

**Military Police Platoon**

**1st Counter Intelligence Corps Det**

**1st Quartermaster Company**

**1st Reconnaissance Troop, Mechanised**

**1st Signal Company**

**1st Medical Battalion**

**1st Engineer Combat Battalion**

Siegen, it became embroiled in the developing Battle for the Ruhr Pocket. This was a vast encircling manoeuvre involving the US Ninth Army in the north and the US 1st Army to the south of the German industrial heartland. The Sieg marked the southern boundary of the pocket, which was defended by elements of Field Marshal Walther Model's Army Group B and other forces. While a fast moving armoured column pushed east and north round the pocket from 29 March to effect the link up with the US Ninth Army in the vicinity of Paderborn, the 1st Division prepared to attack the high ground that overlooked Siegen. This attack took place on the 30th but a greater threat was developing to the east where a German counterattack behind the armoured force heading for Paderborn was developing from the hilly terrain of the Sauerland. The division was pulled back from Siegen and replaced by the US 8th Infantry Division. The 16th Infantry Regiment was rushed to Buren, southwest of Paderborn, and its 1st and 2nd Battalions dug in around Gesehe. The German attack stalled quickly and the US forces sealed all exits from the pocket on the afternoon of 1 April. Inside an area of some 4,000 square miles were some 250,000 men of Model's Army Group B and many other German units.

With the Ruhr Pocket sealed, it was essential to prevent any German relief force coming to its aid from farther east. Allied commanders knew that General Lucht's German Eleventh Army was forming in the Harz Mountains and that to prevent any rescue attempt it had to be neutralised by opening an Allied-defended gap between it and the Ruhr Pocket. Before this could be done, the Weser River, 40 miles east of Paderborn, had to be crossed. The First Army pushed westward on a wide front and on 8 April the 1st Division crossed the Weser. The division's 26th Regiment attacked toward Einbeck following the crossing, while the 16th and 18th Regiments consolidated the bridgehead. Within a few days Lucht's forces would be surrounded in the mountains when US forces reached the Elbe River to the east and consequently the fate of the Ruhr Pocket was sealed. Army Group B surrendered on the 17th. Among the captives were 29 generals and one admiral as well as an estimated 310,000 ordinary soldiers. Model was not among them; he committed suicide on the 21st. While the scale of the Ruhr Pocket victory was being revealed, the 1st Infantry Division was involved in the reduction of the 70,000 Germans holding the Harz Mountains. Any escape

Below: Following the Ardennes Offensive, the Allies pushed on into Germany. This map shows the front lines between 7 February and 28 March 1945.

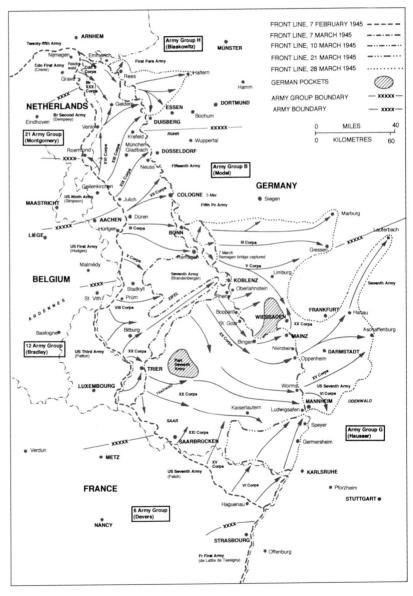

Above: On the look-out for snipers, infantrymen enter a built-up area. *TRH/US Army*

Right: The final days of the war saw Russian and American meet and the Third Reich disintegrate.

routes were sealed off by the middle of April and organised resistance ended on the 22nd.

The speed of the recent advance and the scale of the victories made clear that the war in Europe was almost at an end. However, there was to be no final push by the western Allies on Berlin as they were to hold their positions along the line of the Elbe. The capital of Nazi Germany was to be a Russian prize.

In the final days of the war, the focus of the American advance was southward into southern Germany, northern Czechoslovakia and western Austria. The 1st Division was transferred to the US Third Army for these final operations, an assignment that once again would place it under the command of Patton. The move took the division to the northeast section of the Czechoslovakian border with Germany on 30 April. The thrust into Czechoslovakia was politically sensitive to the Russians and Eisenhower agreed to make only limited inroads into the country. The 1st Division was to make for Karlsbad in the German-speaking Sudetenland that had been taken over by Hitler in September 1938. The operation, which met little opposition, began on 6 May and a day later the war in Europe officially ended. The 1st Infantry Division had come a long way since the beaches of Algeria in November 1942 but had made the bloody and difficult journey to ensure its presence at the end of the Third Reich.

## 1ST INFANTRY DIVISION FORMATION ASSIGNMENTS, EUROPE 1944–1945

| Date | Corps | Army | Army Group |
|---|---|---|---|
| 2 February 1944 | V | First | |
| 15 July 1944 | VII | First | |
| 1 August 1944 | VII | First | 12th* |
| 16 December 1944 | V | First | 12th |
| 20 December 1944 | V | First | 12th/British 21st |
| 18 January 1945 | V | First | 12th |
| 26 January 1945 | XVIII Airborne | First | 12th |
| 12 February 1945 | III | First | 12th |
| 8 March 1945 | VII | First | 12th |
| 27 April 1945 | VIII | First | 12th |
| 30 April 1945 | V | First | 12th |
| 6 May 1945 | | Third | 12th |

\* US 12th Army Group activated on 1st August.

DENMARK

*Baltic Sea*

North Sea

Kiel Canal

KIEL

• ROSTOCK

Rügen

LÜBECK

Wismar

STETTIN

HAMBURG

Wilhelmshaven

Emden

Bremerhaven

Oder

Groningen

Bremen

Elbe

Dannenburg

Dömitz

AMSTERDAM

Wesser

BREMEN

Ülzen

Wittenburg

Lüneberg
Heath

Tangemünde

• BERLIN

NETHERLANDS

Army Group "H"
(Blaskowitz)

OSNABRÜCK

Minden

HANNOVER

US Ninth Army

Twelfth Army

Twenty-fifth Army

ARNHEM

First Para Army

MÖNSTER

Teutoburger Wald

BRUNSWICK

MAGDEBURG

Barby

GERMANY

Cdn First Army
(Crerer)

Hamelin

Eleventh Army

Rosslau

Cottbus

Br Second Army
(Dempsey)

Wesel

Hamm

Paderborn

Harz

Blankenburg

DESSAU

Neisse

US Ninth Army
(Simpson)

ESSEN

DORTMUND

Lippstadt

Leine

Brocken Pk

US First Army

HALLE

21 Army Group
(Montgomery)

DUISBURG

Bochum

Ruhr

KASSEL

Göttingen

Nordhausen

Merseberg

LEIPZIG

Görlitz

DÜSSELDORF

Wuppertal

Sauerland

Army Group "B"
(Model)

Fifteenth Army

COLOGNE

Fifth Pz Army

Marburg

Gotha

Erfurt

Weimar

Zeitz

Colditz

DRESDEN

LIÉGE

Bonn

Sieg

Jena

US Third Army

CHEMNITZ

Remagen

US First Army
(Hodges)

Ohrdruf

BELGIUM

Koblenz

Rhine

Geissen

Fulda

Seventh Army

Thüringian Forest

Hof

Karlsbad

12 Army Group
(Bradley)

Lahn

Seventh Army

Bad Orb

Erzgebirge

PRAGUE

Wiesbaden

FRANKFURT

Hammelburg

Hanau

Schweinfurt

Bayreuth

CZECHOSLOVAKIA

LUXEMBOURG

MAINZ

US Third Army
(Patton)

Oppenheim

Aschaffen
burg

Würzburg

Bamburg

PILSEN

Trier

Worms

Kitzingen

Bohemian Forest

Vltava

Thionville

US Seventh Army
(Patch)

MANNHEIM

NÜREMBURG

Army Group "G"
(Hausser)

Fürth

REGENSBURG

SAARBRÜCKEN

Ansbach

Ceske
Budejovite

6 Army Group
(Devers)

KARLSRUHE

First Army

Heilbronn

US Seventh
Army

Danube

NANCY

Fr First Army
(de Lattre de Tassigny)

Esslingen

STUTTGART

Kirchheim

Donauwörth

Ingolstadt

Landshut

Passau

LINZ

STRASBOURG

Nineteenth
Army

Tübingen

ULM

Dillingen

First Army

Landshut

Inn

Braunau

US Third Army

FRANCE

Colmar

FREIBURG

Landsberg

AUGSBURG

MUNICH

Rosenheim

Salzburg

Berchtesgaden

Enns

BASLE

Memmingen

US Seventh Army

Lake
Constance

Oberammergau

Garmisch

Kufstein

Kitzbühel

AUSTRIA

Füssen

Partenkirchen

SWITZERLAND

INNSBRUCK

Tyrol

Alps

Brenner
Pass

Bolzano

ITALY

US Fifth Army

YUGOSLAVIA

---

- - - - OCCUPIED BY ALLIED FORCES, 28 MARCH 1945
- · - · OCCUPIED BY ALLIED FORCES, 4 APRIL
- - - - OCCUPIED BY ALLIED FORCES, 18 APRIL
· · · · · OCCUPIED BY ALLIED FORCES, 7 MAY

BRITISH ATTACKS
US ATTACKS
FRENCH ATTACKS
GERMAN POCKETS
OCCUPIED BY RUSSIAN FORCES, 16 APRIL

0 — MILES — 120
0 — KILOMETRES — 200

**Above:** After the battle for France the Allies fought through Belgium and Holland — and the Ardennes Offensive — to reach Germany. These are infantrymen of 1st Division's 16th Infantry Regiment (Company F of 2nd Battalion) in the woods of Germany. *US Army via Real War Photos*

**Right:** Just before the German push into the Ardennes — this is Company C, 2nd Battalion, 16th Infantry Regiment in Belgium. *US Army via Real War Photos*

**Opposite, Above:** Company B, 1st Battalion, 16th Regiment moving out from Scheidhausen to cross the River Roer, 25 February 1945. The second man is carrying a BAR (see photo page 6). *US Army via Real War Photos*

**Opposite, Below:** Company A, 1st Battalion, 16th Regiment moving out to cross the River Roer, 25 February 1945. Note the Bazookas (second and third men at left) and ammunition carried by man at right. *US Army via Real War Photos*

**Right:** Company B, 1st Battalion, 16th Regiment crossing the River Roer, 25 February 1945. *US Army via Real War Photos*

**Below:** This photograph shows Company K, 3rd Battalion, 16th Regiment advancing into Germany after crossing the River Roer, Lendersdorf, Germany, 25 February 1945. *US Army via Real War Photos*

**Opposite, Above:** Company F, 2nd Battalion, 16th Regiment moving past an M10 tank destroyer through Weilerwist, 5 March 1945. The M10 is unlikely to be part of the 1st Division's attached armoured units as the 612th TD Battalion had M18 Hellcats and the 741st Tank Battalion would have had M4 Shermans. *US Army via Real War Photos*

**Opposite, Below:** Company E, 2nd Battalion, 26th Regiment preparing to move forward. *US Army via Real War Photos*

**Opposite page, Above:** Troops of Company A, 80th Chemical Brigade set up mortars on the outskirts of Weilerwist, 5 March 1945, while Company H, 2nd Battalion, 16th Infantry Regiment pass by on their way to attack Metternich. *US Army via Real War Photos*

**Opposite page, Below:** Troops of Company I, 26th Infantry, move past Shermans to attack positions outside Bleishheim, 5 March 1945. *US Army via Real War Photos*

**Above:** Riflemen take cover under fire, 13 April 1945. *US Army via Real War Photos*

**Left:** Machine gunners of Company G, 26th Infantry, move out of Weilerwist, 5 March 1945. *US Army via Real War Photos*

# INSIGNIA, CLOTHING & EQUIPMENT

Right: BAR gunner showing the divisional flash on his left shoulder. *Stephen Dean*

Below: The divisional shoulder patch showing the 'Big Red One'. It was worn on the left shoulder unless the wearer had transferred to a new division when they wore their old flash on the right shoulder.

Below Right: The enamelled badges are regimental crests: 16th Infantry Regiment (above left), 18th Infantry Regiment (below) and 26th Infantry Regiment (above right).

As an essentially standard division within the ranks of the US Army, the 1st Infantry Division was very much clothed and equipped as other infantry divisions. Clothing types evolved as new combat uniforms were introduced, but badges of rank and weapons were much the same as those of other units throughout the US Army and remained as they had been before 1941. However, the division did have some specific insignia that identified both its soldiers and larger units as belonging to the 'Big Red One'.

## INSIGNIA

The most famous badge of the 'Big Red One', and from which it gained its nickname, was the divisional emblem. This consisted of a bold red Arabic numeral 1 on an olive green background shield. It was usually worn on the left shoulder, although it was not always displayed in combat and was often removed in billet so as to deny the enemy a potential source of intelligence. In some units the badge might appear on the side of the helmet. During Operation 'Torch', the landings in North Africa in

Above: Reinforcements for Normandy board landing craft at a British port; note the pack and equipment stowage . *Chris Ellis Collection*

Above Right: Fighting in Bizerta, Tunisia, 1942. This gives a good rear view of the equipment carried by infantryman at this period of the war. *Chris Ellis Collection*

Below Right: Advancing into Germany after crossing the Roer River, February 1945. Note trailer and equipment. *Chris Ellis Collection*

November 1942, the division's troops wore a very prominent US flag on the left shoulder of their field jackets to identify clearly the country of their origin in an attempt to prevent the Vichy French from firing on them. Individual units within the division also had their own badges, although these were not usually found in the front line, except on identification boards outside barracks or regimental headquarters. Many were developed within the units themselves. As an example, the 26th Infantry Regiment, known as the 'Blue Spaders', have a badge that consists of a vertical blue arrowhead on a white background in the shape of a shield with a scalloped top edge. The arrowhead is a stylised Native American Mohican arrowhead. The badge was the brainchild of Colonel Hamilton A. Smith, the regiment's commander during 1917–18, and symbolises the regiment's courage, relentless pursuit of the enemy and daring.

A variety of standard rank badges was also worn, although often dispensed with in combat for fear of attracting sniper fire. If worn under such conditions they appeared on the outer ends of the shoulder straps of field jackets. They were sometimes painted on the helmet, usually in white, by junior officers. Officers' badges consisted of a single gold bar for a second lieutenant, a silver bar for a first lieutenant, for a captain two silver bars; while a major was identified by a single gold leaf with seven points. Further up the command chain, a lieutenant-colonel wore a a single silver leaf, again with seven points, while a full colonel's badge consisted of a silver eagle with spread wings carrying a sheaf of arrows in its talons. With regard to enlisted men, badges were worn on both sleeves of the field jackets and chiefly consisted of varying numbers of chevrons with their point uppermost, which were sometimes joined by rockers, semi-circular bands of braid joining the lower points of the chevrons. Privates first class wore a single chevron; corporals two chevrons, and sergeants three chevrons. Above these, a staff sergeant wore three chevrons and one rocker; first sergeants, three chevrons and a pair of rockers with a hollow diamond device positioned in the space between them; and a master sergeant wore three chevrons and three rockers. Men with some form of specialist training were identified by modified versions of the above badges. For example a technician fifth grade wore a corporal's two chevrons but with a large letter T positioned under them. The highest of these ranks was technical sergeant, which earned three chevrons and two rockers. Finally, badges of service in yellow metal were worn by all troops. These appeared on the shirt wearer's left collar and in case of infantry consisted of crossed muskets, while crossed cannon barrels identified artillery.

# CLOTHING

### Early Field Dress and the M1941 Field Jacket

The most common combat equipment worn by US troops in the period from 1941 to 1944 consisted of olive drab trousers made of wool, web gaiters with russet brown ankle boots, and the M1941 field jacket. The field jacket was single-breasted and hip-length, and was made from a heavy cotton cloth. It had a zip fastener that was hidden behind a buttoned fly and a pair of pockets. It colour was officially olive drab but it was more often seen in light buff. Despite its initial popularity, the M1941 jacket was not sufficiently wind- and waterproofed to offset the worst weather of a European winter. The gaiters also proved less than popular as they were difficult and time-consuming to remove. The lack of comfort of some of these items, which were most worn in North Africa and Italy, led to the development of a new combat dress.

**Right:** Thompson .45-cal sub-machine gun resting against the jeep behind him, this re-enactor wears an officer's gold/black-piped garrison cap, an olive drab M1941 jacket and M1938 dismounted leggings. *Stephen Dean*

**Below:** The M1 Thompson fired from the shoulder. Note the five-pocket pouch for 20-round Thompson magazines. These were often used for the 30-round versions when the magazines protruded from the top of the pockets. *Stephen Dean*

**Opposite, Above and Below:** Two more re-enactment views — of Company E of the British commemorative unit of 16th Infantry Regiment. Note the flamethrower in the lower photograph. *Stephen Dean*

Above: The 16th Infantry re-enactors show off their .30-cal machine gun. Note the ammo box, loader and two chevrons on the corporal in charge. *Stephen Dean*

Below: Prewar training photograph of a 1st Division AA gun and crew in action in the New River area of North Carolina during August 1941. Note the British-style M1917A1 helmets that were in production as late as 1940. When war came the M1 swiftly took over. *US Army via Real War Photos*

### M1943 Field Dress

First issued in Italy during 1943, this became the standard dress worn by US troops in northwest Europe during the period 1944–45, although examples of earlier styles were to be seen for six months or more after the D-Day landings. This combat uniform was based on the concept of producing an adaptable design which was meant to be appropriate for summer in its basic form and, by adding other clothing in layers, could serve equally well in winter. The colour of the M1943 Field Dress was a deeper green than the previous M1941 clothing, but the colour did vary from very dark to almost greyish-green. The thigh-length, single-breasted field jacket had a concealed zip fastening and hidden buttons. On the outside were four pockets with pointed flaps and it had a drawstring around the waist. Unlike its predecessor the jacket was designed to be fully wind- and waterproof as well as being more resistant to tearing. Beneath the jacket soldiers tended to wear an olive drab woollen shirt in mild weather, while in colder conditions the shirt was often supplemented by a olive drab woollen sweater. The cold-resisting qualities of the M1943 jacket could be improved by the introduction of a button pile fabric liner and, from 1944, a hood. Trousers were produced in similar material. The old separate webbing gaiter also gradually disappeared during 1944 to be replaced by a new combat boot that laced well up the shin and had a built in leather gaiter or anklet that fastened over the upper part of the boot and was held in place by a pair of buckled straps. Finally, in 1945 a third type of footwear was introduced. Modelled on the footwear worn by US airborne forces, the new boots were one piece and laced up to the calf.

## OTHER CLOTHING

At various times, particularly in cold weather, troops drew on other items of equipment. Both long-length greatcoats and raincoats, the former in a brownish olive green and the latter in a deeper shade. Waterproof ponchos were also made available. Aside from the common olive green brimmed knit cap, better known as the 'beanie', troops were provided with balaclavas and olive green wool scarves. Beanies and balaclavas were often worn under the standard two-piece M1 steel helmet. Among the other types of equipment carried or worn by US troops were water canteens, often seen in a canvas cover, bayonets and combat knives, and an entrenching tool, which was provided with either a fixed or folding shaft. As with many other items of kit, webbing varied considerably in colour, but was usually found in dark green or a light yellow-brown. Other items also commonly seen in many photographs of troops from the period

*Above: Rifleman with an M1 .30-cal Garand rifle.*
*TRH Pictures*

are a wide selection of bandoliers and musette bags. The musette bag was a canvas haversack with a shoulder strap, while the bandoliers were made of cotton and usually divided into five pockets for extra clips of ammunition. Various pouches that could be fitted to the waist belt were available for those men armed with sub-machine guns such as the Thompson and M3, or the Browning Automatic Rifle.

# INFANTRY WEAPONS

### Colt M1911A1
Designed by John Browning in 1900, this automatic pistol remains in service to the present day. It was officially adopted in 1911. A .45-calibre weapon, a seven-round magazine was pushed into the butt and an eighth round could be placed in the chamber over a full magazine. The weapon weighed 2lb 7.5oz.

### Colt M1917
This .45-calibre six-shot revolver saw extensive service in World War I and was superseded by the Browning automatic. However, a shortage of handguns led to some held in reserve being issued in 1941. It weighed 2lb 8oz.

### Smith & Wesson M1917
Adopted in World War I, this six-shot revolver also service in World War II. It weighed 2lb 4oz and was of .45 calibre.

### Springfield M1903A1
Based on components from the Mauser company, from which a licence was purchased in 1903, the Springfield appeared in service during 1905 and soldiered on until the Korean War. Shorter than previous designs, the M1903 was in fact obsolescent by World War II, but did see some service, including as a sniper's rifle. It was a .30-calibre, bolt-action weapon that was fitted with a five-round magazine.

**Above Left:** The GI on the right (pre-December 1941) wears webbing comprising the M1910 haversack in marching order with an M1910 pack carrier containing a blanket roll fitted to the bottom, and a M1918 cartridge belt. His M1939 olive drab (OD) wool service coat is worn over a wool shirt and black tie. The M1937 OD trousers are tucked into M1938 canvas leggings. The M1917 helmet has a leather chinstrap. The rifle is an M1903 .30-cal Springfield. Note leather scabbard for M1905 bayonet. On the left, in early 1942 equipment, the soldier has an M1928 haversack, 'Parsons' field jacket, M1923 cartridge belt, Springfield rifle with 1931 pistol grip, M1910 canteen and M1917A1 helmet with webbing strap. Both men carry M1910 T-handled entrenching tools and, slung over their right shoulder, gas masks. *Tim Hawkins*

**Above Right:** From the 'Torch' period — M1942 herringbone twill jacket and trousers, gas mask on left hip, US flag on a brassard on his left arm, M1928 haversack with M1942 bayonet, M1 helmet and M1 .30-cal semi-automatic rifle. *Tim Hawkins*

**Right:** Closeup of 1942 herringbone twill trousers. The M1910 entrenching tool hangs from an M1928 haversack. From the M1936 belt hangs an M1910 canteen. *Tim Hawkins.*

**Left:** June 1944, and a group of US servicemen are photographed at a Channel port. *TRH Pictures/DoD*

**Below:** Reconstruction of Omaha beach with infantry dragging themselves up from the waterline. The soldiers carry some 70lb of equipment each — although everything feels a lot heavier after wading through the surf, particularly the herringbone twill jacket and trousers, canvas leggings and boots. Their haversacks are M1928s, their M5 assault gas masks are in a black waterproof bag around their necks. Their rifles are protected frim the elements by black plastic covers — these, and the US Navy M1926 lifebelts, were discarded quickly on reaching the beach, accounting for much of the detritus visible in photographs of the landings. The light-coloured materials on the left upper arm were chemically treated brassards that would change colour and provide an immediate visual warning should the German defenders use gas. In the end, neither side did make use of gas as a weapon, although it was stockpiled for retaliatory use. *Tim Hawkins*

### M1 Rifle

A gas-operated automatic rifle, the .30-calibre M1 was better known after i creator, John C. Garand. Adopted in 1936, it quickly became the US Army's standar rifle and four million were manufactured during the conflict. Two sniper's rifles we also available, the M1C and M1D, but only their telescopic sights and flash hoo varied from the original. An eight-round magazine was used in all cases. Patte rightly described the rifle as 'the best battle implement ever devised'.

### Carbine M1

A Winchester company semi-automatic carbine was first offered to the US Army early 1941 but did enter not production until October 1941. Initially designed fe troops who were not combat infantry, the carbine, which had a 15-roun magazine, proved immensely popular and further models followed, including folding stock version designated the M1A1, produced primarily for airborne force The M2 was manufactured as a fully-automatic weapon capable of firing up to 75 rounds per minute from a 30-round magazine. Some seven million carbines we supplied during the conflict.

### Thompson M1 Sub-machine Gun

The first Thompson adopted by the US Army was designated the .45-calibre M192 or 1928A1, but this was complex and a simplified version was adopted in Apr 1942. This, the M1, had a box magazine capacity of 20 or 30 rounds, although th 50-round drum magazine was seen. The maximum rate of five was 700 rounds pe minute.

### M3A1 Sub-machine Gun

Better known as the 'Grease Gun', the M3 was an attempt to mass-produce

impler and lighter weapon than the Thompson. Made mostly from steel stampings, it was a sliding-stock .45-calibre weapon weighing 8.2lb and capable of firing 400 rounds per minute. Manufactured by the Guide Lamp division of General Motors, some 620,000 were produced during the war.

## Browning Automatic Rifle

Developed in World War I, the Browning was a squad gas-operated automatic weapon that had a maximum rate of fire of 550 rounds per minute. Of .30 calibre, it weighed 19.2lb and the ammunition was carried in a 20-round magazine. A bipod was issued to reduce the vibration when fired and therefore improve accuracy. Although the weapon was popular with the troops, it was heavy and clumsy.

## Mark 2 A1 Grenade

Based on a French World War I design, this cast-iron 'pineapple' grenade was fitted with a so-called 'mousetrap' ignition device developed in the interwar period. This consisted of a lever that held down a small spring-loaded arm with a firing pin. When the lever was released the firing pin snapped like a mousetrap and lit the fuse. The grenade was usually filled with smokeless powder rather than high explosive to produce large shrapnel fragments.

## Rocket Launcher 2.26-inch

Better known as the Bazooka, this shoulder-fired weapon fired a hollow-charged finned rocket. The weapon weighed 13.25lb and was 54 inches long. Later versions came apart to ease movement. It first entered service during the 1942–43 North African campaign and proved able to penetrate up to 6 inches of armour.

Left: Soldier from Company A, 1st Battalion, 16th Regiment heading toward the Roer bridge, 25 February 1945. *US Army via Real War Photos*

Below Left: 1st Section, Battery C, 7th Field Artillery preparing to fire its M2 105mm howitzer. This is a postwar shot of troops at Grafenwoehr, today the site of a major US base and range complex. *US Army via Real War Photos*

Below: With gun poised, Sgt Ralph H. Nunn of Knoxville, Tennessee, waits for German paratroops to be flushed out of woods by men of Company M, 3rd Battalion, 16th Regiment. *US Army via Real War Photos*

**Opposite page, Above:** The bocage was a defender's paradise, with sunken roadways and ancient hedgerows dividing small fields — perfect country for anti-tank teams and ambushes. The Allies had to winkle out the opposition with their infantry — here part of a rifle squad. They wear typical equipment — OD field jackets, M1 helmets, leggings and shoes having discarded their heavier kit for this patrol. Note BAR support weapon third in line. *Tim Hawkins*

**Opposite page, Below:** A graphic reconstruction of the D-Day landings. *Tim Hawkins*

**Above:** A reconstruction of a later period — Spring 1945 and the advance into Germany. Supported by an M4 Sherman, this infantry squad is about to clear a German village. The two soldiers in the rear wear M1943 jackets over M1937 light OD wool trousers and M1928 haversacks (note raincoat folded over belt of right-hand man). The man nearest the tank wears a lighter OD jacket. The rear of the tank and the turret is festooned with equipment including ration boxes, packs and ammunition. *Tim Hawkins*

**Left:** World War II saw the proliferation of anti-tank weapons, particularly the development of hand-held hollow-charge equipment such as the US bazooka, British PIAT and German Panzerfaust and Panzerschreck. This is an M9A1 bazooka, three of which were carried by each rifle company's heavy weapons' platoon (along with .30-cal and .50-cal machine guns and three 60mm mortars). *Tim Hawkins*

# PEOPLE

It is perhaps not surprising that ranks of the 1st Infantry Division have been filled with some of these most important figures in recent US military history. Its early service in World War I and its role as one of the country's few regular army formations to remain active in the interwar period ensured that several of those who served with it became renowned during World War II. A few served at the very highest level of the US military establishment during the conflict.

## TERRY DE LA MESA ALLEN (1888–1969)

In 1941 Allen was given command of the 4th Infantry Division after periods in charge of the 3rd Cavalry Brigade and 2nd Cavalry Division between 1940 and his appointment. He then led the 1st Division from August 1942 to August 1943, when both he and his second-in-command, Theodore Roosevelt Jr., were relieved by General Omar Bradley during the Sicily campaign. Bradley's reasons for doing so were complex but he held Allen and Roosevelt responsible for what he later described as: 'The division thought itself exempted from the need for discipline by virtue of its months in the line, and believed itself to be the only division carrying its fair share of the war.' By 14 August Allen was back at General Dwight Eisenhower's headquarters in Algiers

Below: Maj-Gen Terry Allen (second from left), commanding general of the 1st Division, and his staff in Sicily in 1943. Allen and his second in command, Theodore Roosevelt, Jr, were relieved of their commands by Omar Bradley during the Sicily campaign. *US Army via Real War Photos*

and he later received the Legion of Merit for his actions in Sicily during July and August. However, during the late summer of 1943 he returned to the United states where he met General George Marshall, the army's chief of staff. During their discussions an agreement was reached that Allen would take another combat division overseas. In autumn Allen took charge of the 104th Infantry Division, which was training in Arizona, and he set about turning it into an efficient fighting unit. The division moved to Europe in August 1944 and was thrown into the fighting in the Low Countries. In October the 104th became part of the US First Army's VII Corps and by a quirk of fate relieved the 1st Division, which was fighting around Aachen.

# Commanders of the 1st Infantry Division 1938–46

| Name | CO from | To | Comments |
|---|---|---|---|
| Maj-Gen Walter C. Short | January 1938 | January 1940 | Promoted to command US I Corps and later Hawaiian Department but sacked from later position after his poor judgement and dereliction of duty at Pearl Harbor, December 1941 |
| Maj-Gen Karl Truesdell | January 1940 | November 1940 | Promoted to command US VI Corps |
| Maj-Gen Donald C. Cubbison | November 1940 | July 1942 | Promoted commandant of Field Artillery Replacement Training Center, Fort Bragg |
| Maj-Gen Terry de la Mesa Allen | August 1942 | August 1943 | Removed from command in Sicily, later commander of 104th Infantry Division |
| Maj-Gen Clarence R. Huebner | August 1943 | December 1944 | Promoted to command US V Corps |
| Brig-Gen Willard G Wyman | December 1943 | | Acting commander, 7th–14th, previously assistant divisional commander |
| Maj-Gen Clift Andrus | December 1944 | December 1945 | Previously divisional artillery commander |
| Brig-Gen William E. Waters | December 1945 | January 1946 | Previously divisional artillery commander |

Allen retired from the US Army at the end of World War II, but the family's connection with the 1st Division had not ended. His son, Terry Allen Jr, joined the division after graduating from West Point. He became a battalion commander but was killed on 17 October 1967, during the Vietnam War. Two years later his father was injured in a car accident, developed pneumonia and died on 12 September. Father and son are buried at Fort Bliss National Cemetery in El Paso.

# CLARENCE R. HUEBNER (1888–1972)

Huebner was summoned to command the 1st Division in August 1943, a transfer that brought him back into contact with the formation he had served with during World War I. He had been a member of the 18th Infantry Regiment for seven years, rising from private to the rank of sergeant, before he received a regular commission in November 1916. Further promotion followed during the war when he rose to command one of the division's regiments, where he gained a reputation as a no-nonsense disciplinarian. He saw action at Cantigny, Second Battle of the Marne, St. Mihiel and Meuse-Argonne. during this period he gained two Distinguished Service Crosses, a Distinguished Service Medal and a Silver Star. In the interwar period he was attached to Fort Leavenworth's Command and General Staff School (1924) and later was a member of its faculty (1929–33). Before taking over the division, he was the head of the US Army's Ground Forces Staff and Director of Training Service of Supply. During his command of the 'Big Red One', he took part in the Normandy landings and the Allied drive through France to the German border. In December 1944 Huebner was promoted to lead the US V Corps, which had pushed across the Rhine to reach the Elbe by the end of the conflict. Between 1947 and 1947 he was chief of staff US Forces in the US European Theatre of Operations and from 1947 deputy commander-in-chief US European Command. He retired in 1950.

# LESLEY JAMES MCNAIR (1883–1944)

McNair was a career officer who graduated from West Point in 1904 and saw active service in the US occupation of Veracruz, Mexico, in 1914 before joining General John Pershing's punitive expedition into Mexico in pursuit of bandit between March 1916 and February 1917. Following US entry into World War the following April, he arrived in France as a member of the 1st Division. I October 1918 he was promoted to lieutenant-colonel, becoming the younges general officer in the US Army. By the close of the conflict he was the senio artillery officer in the General Staff's Training Section, and spent May to Jun 1919 as commander of the division's 1st Field Artillery Brigade. In the 1920 and 1930s he occupied various administrative posts, taught at the Genera Service School and graduated from the Army War College. From April 1939 to October 1940, McNair was commandant of the Command and General Staff School at Fort Leavenworth and, in the latter part of his tenure, he was acting a the chief of General Headquarters. This body was tasked with mobilising, trainin and reorganising the US Army.

Following US entry into World War II, McNair acted as the chief of the Army Ground Forces and pushed through the various reforms initiated by General George Marshall. In this role he oversaw the expansion of the army from around 800,000 men to its peak strength of 2.2 million soldiers. McNair undertook a number o fact-finding missions and in early 1943 he was badly wounded by shrapnel during a visit to Tunisia. After recuperating, he took over the illusory US 1st Army Group based in England in June 1944, whose bogus radio messages were designed to make the Germans believe that the Allies were about to launch a major amphibiou assault on the Calais region of northern France. After D-Day, he travelled to Franc and during one of his trips to the front shortly before Operation 'Cobra', the US led breakout from the Normandy beachhead, he was killed when US aircra dropped their bombs on his position on 25th July.

Below: George Marshall was an unusual soldier, whose main claim to fame is the postwar Marshall Plan — designed to help the reconstruction of Europe after World War II — that won him a Nobel Peace Prize in 1953. He is seen here (right, wearing cap) with Patton (centre) and General Gaffey, May 1945. *US Army via George Forty*

# GEORGE CATLETT MARSHALL (1880–1959)

Marshall graduated from the Virginia Military Institute in 1901 and saw service during the latter stages of th insurrection in the Philippines in 1902 and 1903. In 1907 he graduated first in his class from Fort Leavenworth's Infantr and Cavalry School and stayed at the base as a member o the army's Staff College until 1908. A series of administrative posts followed in both the Philippines and in both the Western and Eastern Departments back in the United States In June 1917, he reached France as a staff officer with the 1s Division and as its operations officer was instrumental in planning its first attack on the western front at Cantigny in May 1918. He later joined Pershing's staff and was involved in the planning for the St. Mihiel and Meuse-Argonne Offensives. In the interwar period Marshall served as an aide to Pershing, served overseas in China, was commandant o the Infantry School at Fort Benning and took command of th 5th Infantry Brigade.

In July 1938 he was made head of the Army General Staff's War Plans Division and in the following October was rose to the army's chief of staff. In this position he oversaw the vast expansion of the army and created three new commands: Army Ground forces, Army Service Forces and Army Air Forces. He became the main military adviser to President Roosevelt and a key figure in the Allied Joint Chiefs of Staff. In this position he was present at several of the major inter-Allied strategy conference during World War II, not least Casablanca, Cairo, Teheran, Yalta and Potsdam. In 1944 he was promoted to general of the army but resigned his position as chief of staff in November 1945. In 1947, as US Secretary of State he proposed what became known as the Marshall Plan, a program of economic aid to help in the reconstruction of war-damaged Europe. In 1953, he was awarded the Nobel Peace Price, the first soldier of any nation to receive this honour.

# THEODORE ROOSEVELT, JR. (1887–1944)

Born in September 1887, Roosevelt was the son of President Theodore Roosevelt and the nephew of the wartime US president, Franklin D. Roosevelt. During World War I, he commanded the 1st Division's 26th Infantry Regiment and in the interwar period, like his father and uncle, Roosevelt enjoyed a career in politics, as a New York State assemblyman, and an assistant to the Secretary of the Navy. Between 1929 and 1933, he was successively governor-general of Puerto Rico and the Philippines.

Following US entry into World War II, he again took command of the regiment and in 1941 was promoted to be the division's assistant commander. In this capacity he took part in the 'Torch' landings in North Africa during November 1942 and the subsequent battle for Tunisia. After its successful conclusion in May 1943, he took part in the invasion of Sicily the following July, during the opening of which the 1st Division was a spearhead. However, in August, Roosevelt and General Terry

## Congressional Medal of Honor awards

| Name | Unit | Place | Date |
|---|---|---|---|
| Private James W. Reese* | 26th Infantry | Mount Vassillio, Sicily | 5 August 1943 |
| Private Carlton W. Barrett | 18th Infantry | Laurent-sur-Mer, France | 6 June 1944 |
| 1st Lieutenant Jimmie W. Monteith Jr.* | 16th Infantry | Colleville-sur-Mer, France | 6 June 1944 |
| Technician Fifth Grade John J. Pinder Jr.* | 16th Infantry | Colleville-sur-Mer, France | 6 June 1944 |
| Staff Sergeant Walter D. Ehlers | 18th Infantry | Goville, France | 9–10 June 1944 |
| Staff Sergeant Arthur F. Defranzo* | ? | Vaubadon, France | 10 June 1944 |
| Private First Class Gino J. Merli | 18th Infantry | Sars la Bruyere, Belgium | 15 September 1944 |
| Staff Sergeant Joseph E. Schaefer | 18th Infantry | Stolberg, Germany | 24 September 1944 |
| Captain Bobbie E. Brown | 18th Infantry | Aachen, Germany | 8 October 1944 |
| Sergeant Max Thompson | 18th Infantry | Haaren, Germany | 18 October 1944 |
| Technical Sergeant Jake W. Lindsey | 16th Infantry | Hamich, Germany | 16 November 1944 |
| Private First Class Francis X. McGraw * | 26th Infantry | Schevenhutte, Germany | 19 November 1944 |
| Private Robert T. Henry* | 16th Infantry | Luchem, Germany | 3 December 1944 |
| Corporal Henry F. Warner * | 26th infantry | Dom Butgenbach, Belgium | 20–21 December 1944 |
| Staff Sergeant George Peterson* | 18th Infantry | Eisern, Germany | 30 March 1945 |
| 1st Lieutenant Walter J. Will* | 18th Infantry | Eisern, Germany | 30 March 1945 |

* Denotes killed in action.

de la Mesa Allen, the division's commander, were replaced as some senior US commanders believed that discipline in the division was too lax. Whatever the cause of their removal, both officers were highly popular with their men.

Roosevelt spent the remainder of 1943 kicking his heels in Algiers, where he contracted pneumonia shortly before he transferred to England. Roosevelt appealed to General Omar Bradley for some active part in the forthcoming D-Day landings, arguing that his experience in North Africa and Sicily would prove invaluable in Normandy. However, approval was not immediately forthcoming but a written appeal to the commander of the US 4th Infantry Division in May 1944 brought results. He was attached to the division which was scheduled to be the first wave to assault Utah Beach. On D-Day Roosevelt was the first US officer of general rank to reach the beaches and proved a calming and inspiring figure to the men of the 4th Division as they took and moved out from Utah. Roosevelt's steadiness did not go unnoticed. Bradley considered him to be an ideal candidate to command of the 90th Infantry Division and his plan was backed by Eisenhower on the 14th.

Roosevelt never took command of the division. He had succumbed to a heart attack in his sleep the night before. He was buried in a temporary grave in Normandy and among his pallbearers were Bradley, Patton and Huebner, the commander of his old 1st Infantry Division. Roosevelt was subsequently reburied in the formal American Cemetery in Normandy alongside his brother, Quentin. For his action on D-Day, Roosevelt was awarded the Congressional Medal of Honor. The final lines of the citation summed up his role on D-Day: "Under his seasoned, precise, calm, and unfaltering leadership, assault troops reduced beach strongpoints and rapidly moved inland with minimum casualties. He thus contributed substantially to the successful establishment of the beach-head in France".

**Right:** The Medal of Honor is the United States' highest award for valor in action. Awarded to individuals serving in the US armed forces, it is usually presented by the President in the name of Congress — which is why it has become known as the Congressional Medal of Honor. Its origins date back to the US Civil War, when bills were passed for two medals (one naval in December 1861, the other army in February 1862). Since then there have been 3,428 medals awarded., 2,468 to the Army, 649 to the Navy, 294 to Marines, 16 to the Air Force, and one to the Coast Guard.

**Below:** 'We are victorious because we believe in Adolf Hitler and our Greater German Reich' — graffiti above resting men of Company I, 3rd Battalion, 16th Regiment, in Vettweiss towards the end of the war in Europe. *US Army via Real War Photos*

# JIMMIE W. MONTEITH JR.

Members of the 1st Infantry Division won more than a dozen Congressional Medals of Honor during World War II, and one of the most famous went to First Lieutenant Jimmie W. Monteith Jr. of the 16th Infantry Regiment. Monteith was born in Low Moor, Virginia, in June 1917 and won his posthumous award near Colleville-sur-Mer during the fight for Omaha Beach on 6 June 1944. His citation reads:

"…1st Lt Monteith landed with the initial assault waves on the coast of France under heavy enemy fire. Without regard to his own personal safety he continually moved up and down the beach reorganising men for further assault. He then lead the assault over a narrow protective ledge and across the flat, exposed terrain to the comparative safety of a cliff. Retracing his steps across the field to the beach, he moved over to where two tanks were buttoned up and blind under violent enemy artillery and machine-gun fire. Completely exposed to the intense fire, 1st Lt Monteith led the tanks on foot through a minefield and into firing positions. Under his direction several enemy positions were destroyed. He then rejoined his company and under his leadership his men captured an advantageous position on the hill. Supervising the defense of his newly won position against repeated vicious counterattacks, he continued to ignore his own personal safety, repeatedly crossing the 200 to 300 yards of open terrain under enemy fire to strengthen links in his defensive chain. When the enemy succeeded in completely surrounding 1st Lt Monteith and his unit and while leading the fight out of the situation, 1st Lt Monteith was killed by enemy fire. The courage, gallantry, and intrepid leadership displayed by 1st Lt Monteith are worthy of emulation".

# POSTWAR

The conclusion of World War II in May 1945 did not end the involvement of the division in Europe as Allied forces remained in Germany. As the Cold War developed between the Soviet Union and the western Allies after the defeat of Nazi Germany, it became a key component of Nato's forces and remained in what had become West Germany until 1955, when it returned to Fort Riley, Kansas. A further decade was to pass in training and re-equipping before the division became embroiled in overseas combat. In 1965, the 1st Division became one of the first US Army formations to deploy to the Republic of Vietnam to support the country's government against Communist guerrillas, the Viet Cong, who enjoyed the backing of North Vietnam. Advance elements arrived at Qui Nhon on the country's east coast on 23rd June and the main body of the division under Major-General Jonathan O. Seaman began leaving Fort Riley on 15 September, beginning a five-year involvement in the Vietnam War.

## THE DIVISION IN VIETNAM

The early operations by the division involved sweeps, small-scale offensives, and the protection of the country's key highways against attacks by the Viet Cong, not least along Route 13, which became known as Thunder Road due to guerrilla activity along its length. However, by late 1966 the US forces in Vietnam under General William C. Westmoreland were strong enough to undertake large-scale operations involving thousands of troops, particularly in an area of III Corps Tactical Zone to the northwest of Saigon designated War Zone C, where the Viet Cong 9th Division was based. The first of these missions was Operation 'Attleboro', fought between 14 September and 26 November, and the 1st Division was involved in the fighting. Although some 2,000 Viet Cong were reported killed and many others were forced to flee to nearby Cambodia, the enemy quickly resumed their activities in the region, and Westmoreland ordered further offensive sweeps. Operation 'Cedar Falls' was directed against an area known as the Iron Triangle, a zone of dense jungle a little to the south of War Zone C and just 18 miles from the centre of Saigon. The area was a springboard for Viet Cong strikes on the South Vietnamese capital. 'Cedar Falls' began on 8 January 1967, with the 1st Division tasked with sealing off the northern perimeter of the Iron Triangle along a line running from Ben Suc in the north to Ben Cat. A key part of the operation was an helicopter-borne assault by a battalion of the division's 26th Regiment under Lieutenant-Colonel Alexander Haig, later to become one of President Ronald Reagan's secretaries of state, on Ben Suc. Before 'Cedar Falls' ended on the 26th the various US units committed had carried out numerous search and destroy operations that resulted in 750 Viet Cong being killed and 280 captured.

Following 'Cedar Falls', Westmoreland ordered two preliminary operations, 'Gadsden' and 'Tucson', as a diversionary tactic before the commencement of the next large-scale sweep, 'Junction City'. Of the two, the division was committed to Operation 'Tucson' between 14 and 18 February, which involved its 1st and 3rd Brigades deploying into the southeast of the region, some 10 miles south of the village of Minh Thanh, to carry out search-and-destroy missions. However, these tasks were only a cover for 'Junction City', the first phase of which opened on the 22nd. Westmoreland's first intention was to seal off an area in the west of War Zone C, prior to sweeping through the area to destroy North Vietnamese bases and troop concentrations. This involved the division's 1st Brigade in blocking operations along Route 246 east of Katum to seal the border with Cambodia and a push northward along Route 4 by the division's 3rd Brigade to seal off any escape routes to the east. In both cases defensive bases were established and search and destroy missions launched. Most contacts with the enemy involved small numbers but on the morning of the 28th Company B of the 16th Infantry Regiment's, 1st Battalion, ran into major opposition east of Route 4. Despite being almost surrounded in the firefight Company B had beaten off the North Vietnamese by the middle of the afternoon with the aid of artillery and air support. 'Junction City'

continued until 14 May, although contact with the Viet Cong became less and less frequent as many had withdrawn over the border into Cambodia. Nevertheless, some 3,000 Viet Cong had been killed and many of their bases overrun. Having need of troops elsewhere, Westmoreland redeployed the forces committed to War Zone C, and within a few weeks the Viet Cong had moved back into the area.

*Above:* The 1st Division served with distinction in Vietnam for a five-year period from June 1965. *TRH/US Army*

The Viet Cong's Tet Offensive in 1968, although defeated by US forces, marked a turning point in the conflict. Public disenchantment with the war helped to force a re-evaluation of the US commitment in Vietnam. To many, the growing number of US casualties and the seeming resilience of the Viet Cong and North Vietnamese suggested that a meaningful long-term victory could not be achieved. A decision was taken to dramatically reduce the United States' role in the conflict. The division's involvement in the Vietnam War finally end in 1970, when it returned to Fort Riley as part of the Vietnamisation programme, which sought to transfer a much greater share of the ground combat to indigenous forces. In its period in Vietnam, the division had more than 2,000 men killed in action, including one of its commanders, Major-General Keith L. Ware. He and men with him died on 13 September 1968, when his helicopter was downed by ground fire close to Loc Ninh to the north of Saigon. Eleven soldiers from the division had been awarded the Congressional Medal of Honor, while several Meritorious Units Commendations were granted, including Vietnam 1968; The Republic of Vietnam Cross of Gallantry with Palm Streamer embroidered Vietnam, 1965-1968; and First Class Streamer embroidered Vietnam, 1965-1970. It was to

Above: Brig-Gen John R. Deane, assistant CG of 1st Infantry Division, checks his map with 1st Battalion of 18th Infantry during Operation 'Attleboro II', a search and destroy mission in Tay Ninh Province. Note the unchanged 'Big Red One' shoulder patch. *TRH/US Army*

be some 20 years before the division was again to see combat This time not in southeast Asia but in the Middle East.

# WAR IN THE MIDDLE EAST

On 2 August 1990 Saddam Hussein launched Iraqi forces into the neighbouring oil-rich state of Kuwait in the Persian Gulf, an ac of aggression that led to the formation of a world-wide military coalition to liberate Kuwait. As part of the coalition, the division was put on alert for deployment on 8 November, once it had become clear that diplomacy was unable to engineer an Iraqi withdrawal. Over the following eight weeks the division under Major-General Thomas G. Rhame gathered in Saudi Arabia some 12,000 troops and around 7,000 items of equipment as part of the build-up of coalition forces known as Operation 'Desert Shield'. The first stage of the liberation of Kuwait opened at 02.00 hours on 17 January 1991 and involved sustained air attacks, known as Operation 'Desert Storm', against the Iraqi military infrastructure in both Iraq and Kuwait. Air power alone did not force Saddam to withdraw, and the coalition forces under General Norman Schwarzkopf prepared to launch a ground offensive. The coalition forces were arrayed along Saudi Arabia's northern border with Iraq and Kuwait, with the intention of launching a right hook northward through southern Iraq that would take the troops involved to positions north of Kuwait City. The Iraqis would either be surrounded or forced to retreat. For this ground operation, code-named 'Desert Sabre', the division was assigned to the VII Corps, which also included the US 1st and 3rd Armored Divisions, the US 1st Cavalry Division, and the British 1st Armoured Division.

'Desert Sabre' opened at 01.00 hours on 24th February and the Iraqis crumbled quickly. Advancing across the desert the division smashed through the defences being held by the enemy's 26th Infantry Division, taking some 2,500 prisoners, thereby allowing the British 1st Armoured Division to push deeper into southern Iraq. Capitalising on this success, the division switched the axis of its advance eastward and collided with the Tawakalna Division of Saddam's Republican Guard, which was supported by the Iraqi 12th Armoured Division. Fierce fighting ensued during the night of 26–27 February, with the division crushing both enemy formations. Some 40 Iraqi tanks and a similar number of other vehicles were destroyed. Throughout the daylight hours of the 27th the division pushed forward to positions north of Kuwait City, again neutralising pockets of enemy resistance. The 1st Squadron of the 4th Cavalry cut the road leading northward to Iraq and the remainder had taken up holding positions around it by the morning of the 28th. At 08.00 hours, the fighting was brought to an end by a cease-fire. In 100 hours the Iraqi forces had been either destroyed, sent into headlong retreat or were prisoners of the coalition. during this period, the division had advanced some 160 miles of enemy-held territory and Destroyed 550 Iraqi tanks and 480 other vehicles. Iraqi soldiers had also surrendered in their tens of thousands, including 11,500 to the division alone. Some 18 of the division's troops had been killed. On 1 March Safwan Airfield was occupied by the division as part of the ongoing cease-fire negotiations, and over the following months its various units returned home. On 10 May it unfurled its colours at Fort Riley, Kansas. Three new campaign streamers had been added for its participation in the war: Defense of Saudi Arabia, the Liberation of Kuwait, and Cease-Fire.

# REORGANISATION AND BALKAN PEACE-KEEPING

ive years after returning to Fort Riley the division was reorganised as part of sweeping reforms within the US Army. At the centre of these changes was a major redeployment. While the division's 1st Brigade remained stationed at Fort Riley, its other elements were redeployed to Germany as part of the US Army Europe. In Germany, its headquarters are maintained at Würzburg and other units are stationed at nearby camps. The 2nd Brigade is at barracks in Schweinfurt; the 3rd Brigade at Vilseck; the 4th Brigade at Kitzigen and the divisional artillery at Bamberg.

While the Cold War might have ended with the disintegration of the Soviet Union and the collapse of the Warsaw Pact in the late 1980s and early 1990s, the world remained full of tensions, not least between rival ethnic groups within the Balkans. In 1996 elements of the 1st Division became embroiled in one of the most brutal of these conflicts, that between Bosnians, Croatians and Serbians in the former Yugoslavia. Attempts to broker a peace between the warring factions reached fruition in December 1996 with the signing of the Dayton Peace Accord in Paris. The division's 1st Squadron, 4th Cavalry Regiment was involvement in the opening phase of an international peace-keeping effort to Bosnia, entering the country in January 1996 as part of Operation 'Joint Endeavour'. Later the same year, other elements of the division assumed authority and control of Task Force Eagle in a ceremony that took place at Eagle Base on 10 November. The division became the key element in a force that comprised troops from 12 nations and operated in a force area that was designated Multi-National Division North until in October 1997 its role was taken over by the US 1st Armored Division.

The division's experience in Bosnia was to prove highly valuable during its next deployment. On 5 February 1999 it was informed that it would be part of Task Force Falcon, a NATO peace-keeping force to be deployed to Kosovo to separate warring factions. After conducting appropriate exercises in February and March, forward elements moved to Camp Able Sentry in neighbouring Macedonia and on 12 June part of the division entered Kosovo as part of Operation 'Joint Guardian'. Two camps were established — Camp Monteith at Gnjilane and Camp Bondsteel near Urosevac. Both were named after former members of the division who had won the Congressional Medal of Honor, and it was from these bases that the division conducted the delicate task of maintaining peace and order. The mission in Kosovo was to last for the following 12 months. In June 1999, the Schweinfurt-based units of the division that had been deployed returned to their home bases. Kosovo was the division's last active service to date.

Below: 1st Infantry Division M1 Abrams tanks during Operation 'Desert Storm' against Saddam Hussain's Iraqi forces, 25 April 1991. *TRH/US Army*

# ASSESSMENT

It is difficult to measure the value or effectiveness of a unit of some 14,000 men i
a conflict that involved forces numbering in their hundreds of thousands, usual
acting in concert, and there is no readily quantifiable way to assess combat valu
How then should military effectiveness be measured? Should it be in compariso
with the performance of other units from the same army, or with those of allies, 
the enemy? Also, close attention needs to be paid to what is being asked of the un
and perhaps even the nature of the terrain over which it fights. Finally, and mo.
importantly, did the unit succeed in carrying out its orders?

There is little doubt that US commanders recognised the 1st Infantry Divisio
as a key unit in their order of battle during the period from late 1942 until the en
of the war. During this period the 'Big Red One' was involved in actual combat f
something like 300 days, a remarkable figure when one considers the long perioc
of training it also underwent, particularly during the period in Britain between i
departure from Sicily in October 1943 and the opening of D-Day in June 1944. A
mentioned elsewhere Bradley thought it essential to the Allied plans for D-Day, an
Patton, who had had the division under his command during the later stages of th
fighting in Tunisia, was of a similar mind during the build-up to the invasion of Sici
in mid-1943. He stated in his usual forthright manner: 'I want those 1st Divisio
sons of bitches. I won't go without them.' It is also worth remembering that pric
to June 1944, the United States had in fact comparatively few units in Europe tha
had any combat experience at all, thus forcing experienced units to shoulder 
greater part of the war's burden that might normally be expected.

What is also undoubtedly true is tha
the division was called upon three time
to undertake the most difficult of a
military operations—amphibious assault
No army had trained before World War I
for such complex operations and th
weapons and tactics needed had to b
improvised or developed throug
experience. In some respects, th
division was lucky that the landings i
North Africa and, to a lesser extent, i
Sicily, were not immediately opposed a
they proved valuable experience for th
much more formidable undertaking o
D-Day. On D-Day itself, the assault o
Omaha Beach went badly wrong, chiefl

Below: Sgt Mallory J. Yacopine and Sgt Werner W.
Kahl welcome the 100,000th prisoner taken by the
1st Division, Germany, 23 April 1945. *US Army via
Real War Photos*

AMERIKANISCHE
RIE   DIVISION
IHRE    100.000ᵀᴱ
FANGNER

THE·FIRST·INFANTR
HAILS    ITS
PRISONER    OF

due to factors beyond the control or influence of the division. Losses were heavy and for a time it seemed as if the landing would have to be abandoned. Yet the division recovered from the shock and showed uncommon resolve to fight its way off the heavily protected and defended beach and establish a defensive perimeter inland. It is arguable that D-Day itself might have been put in jeopardy if the division had not accomplished its prime mission. Although the landings in North Africa, Sicily and Normandy were not 100 percent successful in terms of what the planners had envisaged, and it is wise to realise that the division had been asked to carry out tasks probably beyond any unit in such circumstances, they were undoubtedly successful enough to form the basis of subsequent victories.

Aside from the type of operation carried out by the division, it is worth looking at the terrain over which it fought. In Tunisia, Sicily and northwest Europe, there is little doubt that it generally favoured the defenders. Tunisia and Sicily involved the division in tough mountain fighting, often in appalling weather conditions, against a well dug-in and determined enemy. While in Europe itself, it was first confronted by the Normandy bocage, which conferred an enormous advantage on the German troops. To make matters worse, the Allied commanders had given little thought to actually preparing their troops for combat in such terrain, because they expected to be well beyond it before the Germans could respond effectively. After Normandy, the division had to fight in the heavily wooded terrain of the Ardennes and around Aachen, both areas posing their own obvious difficulties.

Turning to the enemy that the division encountered, it is true that the Vichy French and Italians were generally not first-class opponents, both being half-hearted in the cause they were supposedly fighting for. It is an altogether different story with the Germans, and here the division faced some of the best units of what most commentators consider to be the finest army of the war. In Tunisia, these included veterans of the Afrika Korps; in Sicily the Hermann Goering Panzer Division, and in Europe several crack formations of either the Waffen SS or the regular army. Tunisia and Sicily were essentially proving grounds for the division, the campaigns in which it gained the essential combat experience that proved so vital after June 1944. Many of these lessons, not least during the Battle of Kasserine, were brutal – but the division was the better for them. It must also be remembered that the 'Big Red One' was first and foremost an infantry division. As such, it lacked some of the equipment to fight certain types of battle. The most glaring deficiencies were the absence of armour and shortages of transport. Particularly in northwest Europe, it relied on detached units from other divisions to provide these elements, but integrating them into the structure of the division in the midst of combat was not always easy. Nevertheless, the problems were generally overcome.

In the final analysis, all that matters in war is victory, preferably with an 'acceptable' level of casualties, and the Allies did win World War II despite the undeniable qualities of much of the Third Reich's armed forces. That they did so was due to the mobilisation of millions of men in the Allied camp and the industrial might of the United States. However, the brunt of combat, the point where the greatest bulk of US industrial power was ultimately directed, was borne by a surprisingly small number of those mobilised. As the campaign histories of North Africa, Sicily and northwest Europe reveal, the men of 1st Infantry Division carried a not inconsiderable share of that burden, thereby living up to the 'Big Red One''s motto: 'No mission too difficult, no sacrifice too great, duty first.'

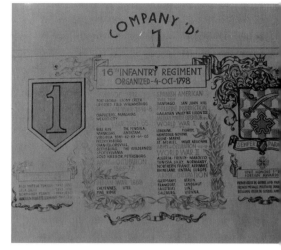

Above: 16th Infantry Regiment's history depicted on a wall of a barracks in Vienna, 1 July 1947. *US Army via Real War Photos.*

## 1st INFANTRY DIVISION IN WORLD WAR II

Casualties
Killed: 4,325
MIA: 1,241
Wounded: 15,457
Total: 21,023

Total days in combat: 443
(89 Africa, 36 Sicily, 318 Europe)

Prisoners of War Taken: 208,000

Awards
Congressional Medal of Honor: 16
Distinguished Service Cross: 161
Distinguished Service Medal: 4
Silver Star: 6,116
Legion of Merit: 79
Bronze Star: 14,138
Soldiers Medal: 162
Air Medal: 76
Total awards: 20,752

# REFERENCE

## INTERNET SITES

http://www.1stdivision.org/
The site of the 1st Infantry Division Military History Group based in Illinois. The site covers many aspects of the division's history and has a regular newsletter.

http://www.ibiblio.org/hyperwar/USA/OOB/1-Division.html
Part of the mammoth Hyperwar US Army in World War II project, this site gives an outline of the 1st Division's order of battle, its commanders, theatres of action and a detailed snapshot of its combat assignments.

http://www.bigredone.org/
The home of the Society of the 1st Infantry Division, which was founded in 1919. The society organises trips and reunions and also sells merchandise commemorating the division.

http://www.army.mil/cmh-pg/documents/eto-ob/1ID-eto-ob.htm
A detailed review of the commanders and staff, composition, casualties, awards, unit attachments and detachments of the division during the period 1943–1945.

http://www.army.mil/cmh-pg/moh1.htm
A site dedicated to recording all of the Congressional Medal of Honor winners from the Civil War to the present. The citation for each winner is available.

http://www.webbuild.net/BeforeTaps/
Before Taps site is dedicated to the story of a 1st Division infantryman, Private First Class Robert A. Baummer, who fought with the division from North Africa to Normandy, where he was killed.

http:/www.rrmtf.org/firstdivision/
The Cantigny First Division Foundation, an organisation dedicated to promote the history of the division.

http://www.strandlab.com/225thmemorial/memsite/1sthistory.html/
A brief overview of the division in World War II.

http://www.bigredone.pwp.blueyonder.co.uk
A British-based group that portrays troops from Coy E, 2nd Bn, 16th Infantry Regt.

ttp://www.geocities.com/bigredoneal/
group of re-enanctors based in Alabama.

ttp://hometown.aol.com/kco16inf/collect/index.htm.
re-enactment group of Company K, 16th Infantry regiment,
ased in Ohio and Pennsylvania.

# BIBLIOGRAPHY

llen, Terry; *A Factual Summary of the Combat Operations
f the 1st Infantry Division in North Africa and Sicily During World War II;* El Paso,
960.
he division's former commander in these campaigns summarises the activities
f his command.

llen, Terry; *Situation and Operation Report of the First Infantry Division During the
eriod of its Overseas Movement, North African and Sicilian Campaigns;* El Paso, 1950.
he former commander recounts the deployment and first actions of the division.

mbrose, Stephen E.; *D-Day, June 6, 1944: The Climactic Battle of World War II;*
ouchstone, 1995.
n excellent telling of the story of D-Day that weaves together the story of those who
ere involved on all sides and at all levels.

lumenson, Martin; *Breakout and Pursuit. United States Army in World War II;*
ashington Government Printing Office, 1961.
fter the slogging match of Normandy, this tells the story of the US-led breakout that
as won through Operation 'Cobra' and the subsequent drive eastward.

radley, Omar; *A Soldier's Story;* Henry Holt and Company, 1951.
he memoirs of one of the most effective US commanders of World
ar II under whom the 1st Division served for much of the conflict.

ole, Hugh M.; *The Ardennes: Battle of the Bulge; United States Army in World War II;*
ashington: Government Printing Office, 1994.
he official history of the defeat of the last great German offensive in northwest Europe
uring the winter of 1944–1945.

rez, Ronald J. (ed); *Voices of D-Day: The Story of the Allied Invasion Told by Those Who
ere There;* Louisiana State University Press, 1994.
irst-hand accounts of all sides involved in the build-up to and fighting on D-Day.

isenhower, Dwight D.; *Crusade in Europe;* Doubleday, 1967.
utobiography of the Allied supreme commander against Nazi Germany.

uller, Samuel; *The Big Red One;* Bantam Books, 1980.
he US director, who served with the division in World War II, tells his story.

.a.; *The First: A Brief History of the 1st Infantry Division, World War II;* Cantigny First
ivision Foundation, Wheaton, Illinois, 1996.
n overview of the division's role in the defeat of Nazi Germany.

## 'Big Red One' Film

A semi-autobiographical movie on the history of the division made by director Sam Fuller (1911–97), who served with the division during World War II. Fuller's film stars Lee Marvin as a World War I veteran leading a squad during the campaigns from North Africa to the end of the war. Released in 1980, it has a running time of 120 minutes.

**Hastings, Max;** *Overlord: D-Day and the Battle for Normandy, 1944;* **Michael Joseph, 1984.**
A readable and analytical history of the battle for France from D-Day to the Allied victo
at the Falaise Pocket.

**Jones, Vincent;** *Operation Torch: Anglo-American Invasions of North Africa;* **Pa**
**Ballantine; 1972.**
An in-depth and well-illustrated overview of the planning and execution of the fir
US operation in the war in Europe.

**Johnson, Willie F. et al;** *First Infantry Division in Vietnam U.S. Army Infantry Divisio*
*1 May 1967–31 December 1968;* **Dai Nippon Printing Co, 1969.**
The story of the latter part of the division's involvement in the Vietnam War.

**Katcher, Philip R.;** *US 1st Infantry Division, 1939-45;* **Osprey Publishing, 1978**
A highly illustrated but compact history of the division.

**Knickerbocker, H. R. et al;** *Danger Forward: The Story of the Fir*
*Division in World War II;* **Albert Love Enterprises, 1947.**
A straightforward history of the division's role in world War II.

**MacDonald, Charles B;** *The Last Offensive; United States Army*
*World War II;* **Washington Government Printing Office, 1990.**
The story of the final days of the battle against the Third Reich.

**Mead, Gary;** *The Doughboys: America and the First World War;* **Alle**
**Lane The Penguin Press, 2000.**
An exhaustive account of the US involvement in World War II. It do
not avoid the friction between the Allied commanders or the problem
of forging the AEF into an effective tool of war.

Top and Above: E Coy 2nd Bn, 16th Regt WW2 re-
enactment unit is a member of the WW2 Living
History Association and can be contacted by e-mail on
mail@1stinfantry.co.uk or by post at 35 Brookfield
Road, Newton Longville, Milton Keynes, MK17 0BP,
England. *Steve Dean*

Below: 1st Infantry Division Memorial at Cantigny.
*Cantigny First Division Foundation*

**Messenger, Charles;** *The Tunisian Campaign;* **Ian Allan Ltd, 1982.**
A highly detailed and well-illustrated overview of the campaign that weaves togethe
extended accounts by front-line troops in a general account of the ebb and flow of battl

**Miller, Russell;** *Nothing Less Than Victory: The Oral History of D-Day;* **Michael Joseph, 1993.**
Hundreds of firsthand accounts telling the story of Operation 'Overlord'.

**Patton, George S.;** *War as I Knew It;* **Houghton Mifflin Company, 1947.**
The memoirs of one of the most controversial and successful US generals of the war.

**Perrett, Geoffrey;** *There's a War to be Won: The United States Army in Worl*
*War II;* **Random House, 1992.**
A look at the US Army as a fighting organisation.

**Rutherford, Ward;** *Kasserine: Baptism of Fire;* **Macdonald and Co., 1970.**
An in-depth look at the campaign in North Africa, focussing on Kasserine

**US Army, Historical Section Staff;** *Omaha Beachhead: June 6–June 13, 194*
**Battery Press, 1984.**
A highly detailed official account of the battle for Omaha and the first wee
of the invasion of Europe.

Whiting, Charles; *First Blood; The Battle of Kasserine Pass, 1943;* Guild Publishing, 1984.

A dramatically written and anecdotal history of the campaign in North Africa that culminates in the first full-scale battle fought by US forces against the Germans.

# MEMORIALS AND MUSEUMS

The most significant memorial to the 1st Infantry Division stands in Washington, DC. Erected thanks to donations from the division's World War I veterans and friends, it was unveiled by President Calvin Coolidge in 1924. The centrepiece of the monument is a gilded statue of winged Victory on top of a column. It was designed by sculptor Daniel Chester French, who was also the creator of the seated figure of President Abraham Lincoln that forms the heart of the Lincoln Memorial. Plaques were positioned around the base of the column to commemorate the 5,516 who died in combat during World War I. They are arranged unit by unit.

In 1955, the memorial was extended by the completion of a terrace and wing on the west side to remember the division's 4,325 men who were killed in World War II. The funds were again raised through private donation and the site was dedicated two years later. In August 1974 a further wing and terrace for the east side was authorised by President Gerald Ford to record the division's 3,079 dead in the Vietnam War. This was formally dedicated in 1977. More recently, in 1995, a granite stone and bronze plaque was added to the east wing to remember the division's 27 dead from the Gulf War. Among those honoured is the 1st Division's first female casualty.

Top and Above: Views inside the excellent 1st Infantry Division Museum at Cantigny. *Cantigny First Division Foundation*

Outside the US and for those with an interest in World War I, there is a small monument to members of the division near the village of Bathelémont in Lorraine, France. It commemorates Privates Thomas Enright and Merle Hay and Corporal James Gresham of Company F of the 16th Infantry Regiment, who became the first members of the AEF to be killed in combat in November 1917. The original monument was destroyed by the Germans during World War II but a new monument was erected after 1945. There is also a memorial in the village of Cantigny, which lies some 65 miles north of Paris. It is administered by the American Battle Monuments Commission and consists of a simple white stone pillar set in parkland. A further point of interest is the village of Fléville in the Champagne-Ardennes region of France. It was liberated by 3rd Battalion of the 16th Infantry Regiment in October 1918 and its coat-of-arms forms the basis for the regiment's badge, which is worn to the present.

The Cantigny First Division Foundation is located in Wheaton, Illinois, on the estate of the late Col Robert R. McCormick, who commanded the division's 1st Battalion, 5th Artillery Regiment, during World War I. The estate contains the First Division Museum, which was officially opened in 1960, and displays material relevant to the division from World War I to the present. The estate also houses the Robert R. McCormick Research Center, which provides resources for the study of both the division and military history in general. The foundation publishes books and other research sources.

# INDEX